AF538301

ADVANCE PRAISE FOR HIDDEN IN PAIN

The mystery of transformation insists that we honor the depths as well as the heights of experience. The painful process of healing contains the paradox that we must first accept the wounds from our past and for a time even allow ourselves to become immersed in them in order ultimately to become free of them. *Hidden in Pain* is about transformation and healing, both for the author as well as for the reader.

Jeanne's story offers each of us an encounter with the magic of relatedness, thus fulfilling in part her vision of the web of connection that exists through all of creation. Disconnection, isolation, and alienation cannot stand as we engage with her story. My personal story is expanded and deepened, as Jeanne's experience becomes a part of my own journey.

Hidden in Pain touches us at the deepest level—at the level of the journey into Christ, a journey that includes suffering. Each of us must submit to the cross in following Him. Jeanne's story demonstrates that we are not alone. Our Lord is with us and reaches to us in our waking reality as well as through our dreams. Thank you, Jeanne, for sharing the dark as well as the light in your journey. As the meaning of your name implies, God's grace truly is with you and manifests to others through you.

Carol Sheffield Greene, Ph.D., Clinical Psychologist, Spiritual Director and Co-Director, Center for Christian Healing of the Episcopal Diocese of Dallas, Texas

"In writing Hidden in Pain, Jeanne Miller captures and models for us that universal process of healing that moves us out of victim-hood through forgiveness and growth into the full life God intends for each of us. With honesty and personal accountability she traces her movement from "Why me?" to "What am I to learn from this?" to "God, what are you and I going to co-create?" Listen to her life; it is a clear testament to the holistic workings of body, mind and spirit."

Mary Ann Reed, PhD. Our Space: Healing, Growth, Creativity Center, Dallas, Texas

"I found it hard to sum up Jeanne's book in just a few words or sentences. They hardly seem to do it justice. I think about all she went through in her extraordinary inner life of visions, path finding, illumination, and pushing through the pain, *and* I know the incredible fact that she was still able to carry on an active outer life of service to others at the same time! Amazing! Unwanted before birth and burdened with disabilities, abuse, and addiction, by all rights Mrs. Miller should have been swept away in loss, grief, disillusionment, and pain. Instead, she passionately chronicles how the human spirit is transformed through a stormy love relationship with God, courageously recounting her journey as a testimony to hope for all who suffer."

Deborah Cover, MS, LMHC, and Spiritual Director (Indiana)

"Having been a past victim of abuse of many forms, Jeanne transcends the common tendency—of us mere mortals—to hate others though they "do not know what they do." With incredible skill, she shares with us glimpses into a depressed mind and soul, chronicling the painful progression of disease and divorce with each their own horrendous emotional toll. Then Jeanne triumphantly draws us into her humbled heart through her courageous determination to help others. In her earnest search, through chaos, for God, Jeanne finds "the peace that transcends all understanding" as only Jesus Christ can give.

I recommend this book to anyone struggling with divorce, past abuse or the chronic pain of progressive disease."

Jill M. Hutchins, MS, LPC.

"Jeanne G. Miller—a truly amazing woman. Professionally, she is respected as a gifted psychotherapist. Personally, she is more than just a survivor; she is an encourager and one who challenges you to examine your own life. After reading of Jeanne's amazing journey, I have an even deeper appreciation for her as a gifted helper, a story-teller, a seeker of wisdom, and a friend."

Kay Reed, MSSW, LCSW.

"The only way to avoid having your life changed by this book is to never pick it up in the first place. No matter who you are or what life has dealt you or your loved ones, Jeanne G. Miller's amazing, heart wrenching story will touch you and speak to your very soul. She has either directly or indirectly experienced a majority of life's horrific struggles and shares them with the reader. On the other hand, she also leaves us with a refreshing and uplifting hope for resolution and transformation of our lives, our eternity, and ourselves."

Christi Lloyd, MSSW, LCSW.

"This life story by Jeanne G. Miller is not the usual "personal testimony" memoir. Mrs. Miller draws the reader into the agonies, challenges, and triumphs of her life as dyslexic, physically challenged, an adopted child, and alcoholic adult. The pain lingers in our minds, carrying us back into the misery of our own childhoods, the disappointments of our lives, and the addictions we have overcome or need to overcome. Her story reminds us of the redemptive potential of these harrowing experiences.

This book is more than a life story. Mrs. Miller is a practicing psychotherapist and Spiritual Director who shares her unique insight into her own struggles, as well as the stories of her clients. In the end, she challenges each of us that it is our turn to consider our stories and to share them with others, giving concrete suggestions about how to do it.

At one point, Mrs. Miller admits, "hell can be experienced on earth." Yet amid the doubts that God cares what happens to her, she finds hidden in the pain the Christ who is there for her."

Jane Purtle, BA. Contributor to *Spiritual Autographs*

"The Jeanne that I know today has a quiet, gracious demeanor that is unmistakably founded on inner strength and oneness with self. The details of insecurity, fears of inadequacy and struggling faith so poignantly described in her book are not apparent in her life today. It is obvious that she found the healing that she sought."

Lou Ann Berman, PhD.

"Jeanne G. Miller has courageously written of her struggles with physical and psychological pain leading her to spiritual openness and healing. Her book also shows how she has integrated personal history into the counseling experience. I recommend this book to anyone who is facing struggles of his or her own and especially those who are involved in pastoral or physiological counseling."

The Reverend Deacon Stephen B. Stine,
Christ Episcopal Church, Tyler, Texas

HIDDEN *in* PAIN

HIDDEN *in* PAIN

a life story of
PERSONAL TRANSFORMATION

JEANNE G. MILLER, MSW, LCSW

Tate Publishing *& Enterprises*

Tate Publishing
& Enterprises

Hidden in Pain: a life story of Personal Transformation

Visit www.tatepublishing.com for more information.

Cover design by Taylor Rauschkolb
Interior design by Lindsay B. Behrens

Published in the United States of America

ISBN: 1-5988645-7-2
06.11.27

ACKNOWLEDGEMENTS

I want to express warm appreciation to my husband, Dolph, whose support and encouragement sustains me. I am grateful to my children who continue to stand by me with support and love. I give thanks to my parents for their love and guidance. I give thanks to my friends and siblings for their love. I give thanks for the wisdom from trained professionals who have guided me through the narrow paths of healing. I am grateful to all those who read my manuscript and either wrote an endorsement or provided suggestions, especially Carol, Mary Emily and Jane. I give thanks to my birth mother for giving to me the gift of life. I give thanks to God who has never abandoned me. I also give God thanks for the gift of His Son who walks with me, especially in places where no one else would go.

FOREWORD

Jeanne Miller is a clinical social worker living and working in the East Texas city of Tyler, Texas. I am one of the Episcopal priests that she mentions in this narrative, and so perhaps I know more than some others of her struggle to "overcome adversity and fulfill God's purpose," to paraphrase *The Book of Common Prayer.* To me, Jeanne is a real embodiment of the archetype of the "wounded healer."

The author was adopted into an upper middle class Texas family soon after the ending of World War II. It was a family that gradually became dysfunctional during the years of her childhood. Early on, Jeanne began to exhibit what have often been termed, unfortunately, as "birth defects," among which were dyslexia and a serious hip displacement. Her increasing disability and pain seemed to defy the physicians.

This book is not just a narrative about a faith journey into a condition of being physically, emotionally, and spiritually made whole, (which it is, of course). Rather, it is a kind of love letter to the reader, a love letter teaching us about life, itself. It would be unfortunate, therefore, if the reader were to see the intent of this book as only an ordinary commentary on herself, and that she simply learned how to live properly by means of her sufferings. Facing her suffering, stoically, is certainly present in the author's life story. What comes through so effectively is the redemptive power of her suffering, and how this power is available to everyone.

Jeanne will draw the reader into deep places of his or her own afflictions through the details of the terrible pain of repeated treatments that often seemed to fail. How would you or I respond if we were in her place? She was tempted on many occasions to lose her faith in God. Would you or I cave in and curse the creator? Those questions followed me as I read her manuscript, and its joyful conclusion enabled me to share, as well, in the forgiveness that she had so deeply needed and wished for.

May you, dear reader, find the steps of your own pathway through life made lighter as you enter into what can only be termed a true healing of the human spirit.

The Reverend Gene Baker, MDiv, MSSW.
Dallas, Texas

TABLE OF CONTENTS

AUTHOR'S NOTE - PASSION TO WRITE

Writing the story of my life had been a passion of mine for many years. I was afraid I would not be able to put on paper in a succinct and meaningful way the events of my life with the feelings and the decisions that went with those events. I would surrender to an ancient voice within telling me all sorts of reasons why I would not be able to put my story into words. Embarrassment, inadequacy, and shame resurrected their buried heads. I was afraid to risk being vulnerable and exposing the things that were hidden in the closets of my life. I would find all sorts of excuses to postpone the actual beginning to write about my life in manuscript form.

Yet, there was this gnawing in my heart that kept getting stronger. I had to put forth more and more energy to suppress the calling. The gentle nudging became a burning passion and then increased to an out-of-control wild fire, and I was unable any longer to fight the desire to write. I began to panic because I did not feel confident in my literary skills to produce a manuscript that would be well written enough to be published. I feared what other people might think, and I feared being exposed if I were really honest about my life. All of the challenges I had gone through tested my limits. Could I and would I now go beyond those limits into the unknown in the writing of this manuscript?

As is the pattern of my life, when God's hand is calling me to a direction He wants me to go, He sustains the pressure in my heart until I choose His will. With fear and trembling, I surrendered to His command to write my story, and so I began to write.

I share my story with you as an example of wounds, scars, and healing. The person that I have come to be has been transformed through the pain of those wounds. I wrote my life's story from my perspective as I remembered the details. I focused on the events and feelings I hid from others. In no way do I wish to discredit the memory of my family or friends or to bear false witness against anyone. I mention important people and events because of their effect on my formation. I have changed the names of my family members and early childhood friends to protect their identity. The important point is this: it is my reaction to them, not their names. I also share my story because remembering my life honors the one who created me.

I believe my story is a living example of the blessings and the gifts of healing and wholeness that life has offered to me. I have experienced a gracious hand moving my life in many directions that led to various types of healing paths. As I have walked through the struggles, the relationships with people, the experiences, the choices, and the sometimes negative consequences thereof, I have learned that nothing has been wasted. I am certain of the truth that all choices have led and will continue to lead me to become the person I was intended to be.

I am reminded, in a maze, there are dead ends that require one to turn around and possibly backtrack. There are many possible paths once I enter the maze. Wrong turns and blind alleys are common. So is getting lost or disoriented. Whereas mazes are mental, linear, left-brained experiences, a labyrinth's path is soothing, rhythmic, and meditative.

A labyrinth is different in that all experiences are part of the entirety of the whole journey. To walk the labyrinth's path, it is necessary for me to follow a path through an intricate pattern until I reached the center. Once reaching the center, I go back out in the same manner. The center of the labyrinth is where I discover the answers to the questions that I am asking. In psychotherapy terms, it is the discovery of the self. Life for me is the labyrinth. This book is about my journey inward and back out again.

Every event that I experienced, every choice that I make, and every emotion that I feel are all part of the ever-developing master plan. Looking back into my past gave me an opportunity to honestly face my life and to make changes where required. When I was stubborn or too fearful to look at a given situation, I found I increased my misery and many times the misery of others. Sometimes life presented events I did not choose. How I responded to those times was my choice. When I allowed the healing process to evolve, transformation could occur in ways that were mysterious and beyond joyful. The joy came only after the hardship of facing the pain.

As a psychotherapist, as a spiritual director, and as a pastoral care assistant, I have heard story after story about how alone a person feels when he or she is going through a difficult passage. In the pages of this book, you will read a few other stories that have been shared with me as examples of his or her struggles—the identity of those mentioned has been camouflaged for their protection. It takes courage to reach out and share something personal, especially when one feels that no one else has ever felt the intensity of his or her pain. There is fear in the unknown, fear that often becomes overwhelming, almost destroying one's ability to form words that describe the event or the feelings.

Everyone has a story to tell about his or her life. While the events of those lives may be similar to one another, the combination of events and of the people surrounding an event makes each story unique. The way something happened, how it was perceived and other variables make every life different. We all have experienced events that have helped to form the course of our life's path. While these details may differ, the emotions and the struggles of the person make each life a story worth telling.

In my own life and from the stories that I have been told, there came a time when in life there was an event or an insight that brought us to our knees. I call this humbling event a *wake up call.* These events or insights trigger the search for answers to questions such as: Why am I here? Who am I? Why did this happen to me? Is there something greater than myself? What do I believe about life and my faith? Is there a God, and if so who or what is it?

The questions themselves produced a kind of a crisis. Some people are born asking these questions. However you arrive at the point in your life when your search begins, there is the opportunity to discover wholeness and a higher calling for your life. Coming face to face with oneself can be earth shattering. Searching one's soul to find its true identity and to find the answers to the questions takes courage. When understanding is found, it takes courage to stay in the search that might take a lifetime. The search is not only in the perception of or in the problem itself but also in the body, the emotions and in the faith. The struggles are numerous.

At times, it may seem like giving up is the only way to stop the pain. Feeling exposed can cause a profound need to try to cover up again. The excuses to stop are endless. Change in and of itself causes a crisis. Those significant persons in your life are also influenced by your change. Because of their own uncomfortable feelings about the changes they see in you, they may attempt to create an environment so that you can return to the old familiarity with them. Are the pain and the confusion that are experienced in discovery and growth worth it? *Yes.*

"Why?" you might ask.

Seeing and accepting the truth that is found through self-awareness has the potential to set us free to live unchained to others or our past. Free to embrace the person that we were designed to be. For me, the influences of early childhood overflowed into adulthood. I emotionally hid from that little girl and symbolically hid her in the closet. I neglected her by trying to run away from all the hurts. I ran because I had no human contact to help me along the way. God the Father became the friend who sustained that lonely little girl and raised her into womanhood where she could rediscover the child's pain. I was so focused on surviving all the different challenges that I lost sight of my talents and innate potential. They remained hidden from me until the challenges were resolved, at which time I awoke to discover the Jeanne that had always been there. Healing of my childhood and the effects those wounds had in adulthood allowed me to be at one with myself. The warring inside has ended. The running has ceased. The hiding has turned into openness. These changes allow me to risk using the talents that I was born with and to celebrate the life that I was given.

Finally, I share my life story of personal transformation and the insights I have gained with you, the reader, as an encouragement should you need to move through any painful situation that requires that you come out of the dark closets of your life to find your radiant healing.

1

STARTING AT THE BEGINNING

Mother and Dad had been married for almost ten years when they decided to adopt children. Martha, their first, was born in 1946. Martha became queen of the household for a year and a half before I arrived. She was the first grandchild as well as the first great-grandchild on my father's side of the family. She was doted over by parents, grandparents, great-grandparents, relatives, and my parents' friends.

I was born in Azle, Texas, in 1947 to a birth mother who was emotionally and financially unable to continue to care for me. I was seven months old when she decided to relinquish her parental rights. Esther, a social worker from the Fort Worth area, knew about Mother and Dad's intent to adopt other children. Therefore, she called them to offer my placement with them.

Mother had no time to prepare my sister for a new baby. There was no time to wean Martha out of her high chair or baby bed. In a hurry, Mother and Dad drove to Fort Worth to meet Esther at a designated hotel room. Dad said later that when he and mother came into the room, he saw me sitting in Esther's lap. I looked up at him, smiling from ear to ear, let out a squeal of delight and reached out to him with both my arms opened wide. He said that he melted in love, picked me up into his arms and emotionally bonded with me forever more.

It was dinnertime when we arrived at my new home. Mother told me that I was placed in my sister's high chair to have my meal. There were so many new things to see and new people to get used to in my new environment. I had finally calmed down enough to begin eating when my sister came into the room and noticed that I was in *her* high chair. Martha ran across the kitchen over to the chair and began beating on me. She got more intense, shaking the chair until it tumbled over and hit the floor. That did not stop her from expressing her disapproval. It took adult intervention to separate us. Mother said the scuffle ended with my sister mad. I was frightened, bruised, and crying. To possibly avoid any further mishaps, Mother felt that it would be wise to place my baby bed, which was Martha's, in the front hall of our home. Later, when Martha had time to adjust to having a new sister in the family, I would be moved to share her bedroom.

Mother found it exhausting to take care of both of her children. My sister and I were only a year apart in age, so to conserve her energy, Mother made Martha and I do most things together. We were dressed alike, and where one went the other went. Mother needed a daily time-out from us, so she would put us down for a nap and go to her room for a private get away. Mother told the story about one particular afternoon when I was unusually energetic. She needed her time out, but I was not compliant—I was still in the baby bed located in the front hall. My bed was made of wire mesh held together by a wood frame. There was a wire top on the bed that could be latched down.

On this particular day, I was wide-awake, and Mother was tired as usual, so she put me down anyway. She gave me my naptime bottle, and *latched* me in. I was *not* sleepy, and there was nothing to entertain me. I began to cry. Then I began to cry *louder.* Then I began to cry with a *scream.* As time went along, I became increasingly angry. Nevertheless, no one came to see about me. To continue my attempts to get attention and to get out of the cage, I started hitting my glass baby bottle on the wood frame as I screamed. I became so angry that I hit and hit and hit the bottle on the side of the bed until it *broke* into pieces. Still, no one came. I cried myself to sleep in a pile of shattered glass.

Mother had a deep abiding faith that faithfully sustained her. It was her wish to pass on to her children the knowledge and the blessings of God's grace. Our family went to the Episcopal Church. I was baptized into the church soon after I was adopted. Mother and Dad gave me the name Jeanne Terrell after a friend of Mother's, who she greatly admired. Jeanne means "God's Grace." Baptism represents the beginning of our lives as Christians, when we are "sealed as Christ's own forever." My parents dedicated me to the service of God, and I would later make my own profession of faith when I came of age.

Home life became very busy. As well as playing second violin in the local symphony, Mother was an accomplished pianist. She was committed to her duplicate bridge afternoons and her tennis lessons. She was involved with her church community. She also volunteered on various community service projects, committees and their governing boards. She actively served as a state delegate for her political party at both the state and national conventions.

A college graduate, Mother believed in scholastic excellence as a goal to be accomplished. She was beautiful, gracious, and full of compassion. She chose a life of service to her community and to others. She gave her money away in the form of gifts to persons, organizations and worthy causes. She put persons whom she felt would appreciate the education through school when their personal funds were lacking. She gave of her own money to begin an Episcopal elementary school. She always enjoyed having her friends drop in for a visit. Her friends and anyone who met mother found it easy to admire and to love her. She was an example of graciousness.

She believed in keeping the peace at whatever cost was necessary. Victorian in nature, she held in her emotions, never talking about them. She had a healthy self-esteem, which may have hindered her ability to relate to me. Her extremely positive outlook, however, brought about in me the feelings of not being able to measure up to her.

Dad was funny, a University of Texas graduate, and witty. He loved to play tennis, to fish as well as to read. In his early business career, he had been part of his family's business and as a pilot for an airline. After the family sold the business and he was no longer employed as a pilot, he purchased a private airplane and farmland. He loved to fly his plane. He would take us places, and it was always an adventure to remember. He was wise and had an uncanny ability to read a person's intent. He loved his close friends and loved to tease them. He was an active member of the local Rotary Club. He loved nature and open spaces. He was a successful provider for the family; however, he lacked a healthy self-esteem to accept his successes. He had mood swings that led to depression and irrational behaviors. Eventually, he became trapped in the cycle of alcoholism.

Dad raised cattle and grew rice on the land that he had bought. One bright sunny afternoon when I was four years old (1951), our parents took Martha and me out to the family farm for Dad to finish his chores. He loaded the flatbed trailer with bales of hay to feed the cattle. He hooked the trailer to the tractor and off we all went. My mother, Martha, and I were riding on the back of a flatbed. We were absorbed in the thrill of seeing the butterflies fly about and the red hawks flying in circles above our heads. We could hear their cries in the wind. The gentle breeze kept us cool as we rode along on the property.

Dad stopped the tractor and my parents went for a walk, leaving Martha and me alone on the flatbed. We sat on the bales of hay pretending we were queens in a pageant, perched high on our thrones. We acted out the crowning of ourselves as queens and pretended to give commands from our throne. My dad's mean Brahma bull spied the hay and decided to charge quickly toward us. From a distance, we heard our dad shouting and waving his hands as he frantically ran toward the flatbed. Martha began to scream hysterically. A warning bell must have gone off in me, too, as I heard my dad shouting and saw the bull picking up speed as he ran in our direction.

I jumped off my throne, picked up a shovel and, as the bull approached, I hit the bull squarely in the front of his head, stunning him for a few seconds. Dad had time to get to the flatbed and save us from the bull. I was a heroine that day and would forever be called upon to attempt to solve some of the family's problems. I grew to believe that I had to carry their burdens and that I would let the entire family down if I did not carry them. In order to be the family hero, I needed to be an adult long before I was emotionally ready. An overwhelming sense of inadequacy grew as I attempted to fill a role I was not developmentally ready to accept.

I remember two other events also when I was four, that helped shape my life, but opposite in nature to the bull story. One afternoon when I was playing with Martha, we were co-contractors building a tower out of blocks that balanced on the windowsill by my bed. The bed was parallel to the wall, and the window was toward the foot of my bed. Martha and I still shared a room and her bed did not have a windowsill. She positioned herself at the head of the bed and I toward the end. As the construction of our castle got larger and more complicated, she kept nudging me down further toward the end so that she could add more blocks. All of a sudden, I fell off the end of my bed, hitting a desk and ripping the corner of my face open before I crashed to the floor. Blood gushed everywhere. I screamed with fear and ran for Mother. When she saw the blood, she quickly gathered me up and rushed me to the pediatrician's office. After getting the blood to stop, it was determined that I needed a plastic surgeon to sew me back together in a way that would not leave an ugly scar. The tear went from the side of my mouth across the face toward the lower jaw.

The repair surgery was a routine procedure for the medical team. However, my experience of it was a nightmare and left scars in my emotions. Mother told me that she could hear me screaming all the way down the hall beyond the double doors leading to the surgery rooms. She could hear me crying even when I was out of sight. The event intensified when I was taken into the cold sterile operating room, full of tools and things I had never seen before. I was asked to lie down on my back on a cold table. The big bright light, which hung from the ceiling, blinded my eyes. I could hear noises I could not identify. I could hear the people in the room talking to each other. The nurse would not let me up to look around and see what all the noise was. I became paralyzed with fear. Without a warning, someone placed an ether mask down on my face (eyes, nose, mouth and all). My eyes burned, and all I could breathe was a strong odor that burned my throat and eyes. I gasped for clean air to breathe. I screamed, fought for my freedom and kicked the nurse to get loose. She held me down with force to keep me from hurting her or myself. I remember screaming and fighting for my *life and freedom* until I fell asleep.

A few months later I needed my tonsils removed, and I again was put to sleep with the ether mask placed over my face. Once in the operating room, I suspected that something was terribly familiar about being in there. I had learned that trusting a stranger in hospitals was dangerous, so I started to the fight sooner. I began to scream bloody murder and fight the nurse. This time the nurse understood my fright and before she placed the mask on my face, she helped me to understand that everything was going to be all right. Then she gently placed the mask over my nose.

Toward the end of that same year, Mother and Dad told Martha and me we were adopted. Mother had a book about being a "chosen" baby and how that was different from a "natural" baby. Mother began reading the book to us to educate us about what it means to be a "chosen" baby. The book also helped to prepared children for the addition of another baby that was biologically the same as the parent. Mother was pregnant and she wanted to prepare us for the birth of another sibling. Chosen was good. It meant that I was wanted.

Vacations were needed as a break from the business of the family duties. We began to go out of state, renting the same house in the same town for the same month every the year. We were a happy family during that month. There was more time for my parents to pay attention to us. We would go on picnics, wade in the streams, visit near by cities. I grew to love the Colorado Mountains and the fresh clean cool air. For me it was heaven and a place for my personal renewal.

2

WHAT IS WRONG WITH ME? WILL NEW SKILLS HELP?

It was fun being five-years old. My brother, Chad, was born the day before my birthday, making my day more eventful. The house was buzzing with extra relatives bringing presents for Chad and for me. Dad took Martha and me to the hospital to visit Mother. We were too young to go up to the second floor to see Mother, so her nurse brought our baby brother down to us. We could see him through the glass doors of the old fashioned elevator. I remember seeing Dad smile, and his eyes lit up with happiness. It was a special time for all the family.

I began kindergarten that same year. The best part of the day was after nap. We were given cookies and milk before continuing our activities of playing, exploring, and learning to read letters and pronounce the sounds of those letters. We then learned to put those sounds into words. At the end of the year, the teacher told Mother she was concerned that I had not begun to process letters as readily as the other students. She advised Mother to watch my progress closely, as I tended to switch letters and to write them backwards more often than was normal for my stage of development.

There were so many more children in the first grade. The building had several stories and many rooms. It was so much fun. The playground was full of swings, slides, and jungle gyms for exercise. First grade was fun until learning to read became more difficult.

In kindergarten, the teacher taught reading using phonics. But now, the first-grade teacher taught us using flash cards with whole words for us to memorize. To remember the word, I had to see all the letters in their proper order and decipher what it meant. My brain needed extra time to process this new method. I was not given the extra time I needed, yet I was expected to keep up with my classmates. I soon began to fall behind.

The teacher did not understand my special needs. The number of times I saw the letters backwards began to increase. The more mistakes I made, the more self-conscious I became. The more aware I became of my mistakes, the more anxious I was. Holding my train of thought was difficult. Many times, as I was talking, my mind would go blank and my thoughts would disappear. Because I felt so embarrassed, it was difficult to reclaim the thoughts or the words. I was mortified, and I felt so *different* from everyone else.

My handwriting was a mess. I added extra letters that did not belong. I left out necessary ones. I even reversed letters and numbers. At times, my handwriting would consolidate letters to make a word that had no meaning. I needed extra time to process the thoughts into usable information. Another idiosyncrasy was that my brain would sometimes picture an answer before the words could form. If that happened the spoken word would come out all scrambled.

I made so many mistakes. Why was I so different? What was wrong with me that I could not perform like the other students? Why did the teacher pick on me? I felt so *inadequate.* I believed that other students, and certainly the teacher, thought I was inadequate. I felt guilty because I sensed that my teacher was holding me responsible for not succeeding.

As the year progressed, the students began to make fun of my mistakes. I was afraid I would make a mistake even before it happened. The teacher began to treat me as though I was not trying and I felt her impatience toward me. I remember that she would sit me on a high stool in the corner of the room for not paying attention or not trying. I was trying my very best. My best was not good enough. I was confused and lonely. The high stool, where I was placed, was above all the other students' desks, and everyone saw me sitting there. I felt *shame* for the first time in my life.

My mother conferred with my former kindergarten teacher about the difficulties that I was experiencing in the first grade. The teacher suggested that Mother find a copy of the McGuffey reader series for Mother to use as homework to help increase my familiarity with words and reading. The McGuffey readers were written to inspire high scholastic standards in the areas of grammar, vocabulary, and reading.

Mother would read bedtime stories to Martha and me. This was a fun time as we all gathered together. As an alternative to reading, mother would sometimes play on the piano bedtime stories that were written to music. We had fun singing along. However, when she would make me read aloud from the McGuffey reader instead of hearing a bedtime story, I would sink in shame. I made so many mistakes pronouncing the words and remembering their meaning. Mother tried her best to help me. School, as well as the McGuffey reader, was beyond my comprehension.

When I was seven-years-old, I would sneak into my parents' room after they went to sleep. I needed to be close to them to feel security, comfort, and acceptance. I would sleep on the couch in their bedroom, snuggled under the couch cushions. The cushions hid my presence in case they woke in the middle of the night. I would sneak back into my bedroom just as the sun was coming up.

My third-grade teacher was a work of cruelty. I was inquisitive, quick to learn new information by experience; but I was exceptionally slow to read or to learn from books. I continued to write backwards, leaving out words or letters and condensing sentences into strange combinations of letters that, in my mind's eye, was a complete sentence. My mind worked faster than my hand could write. I had the same problem with talking. I became the class scapegoat, a child who did not pay attention and did not want to try to learn. In response, shame continued to overshadow my actions.

I developed self-doubt about what I could do. I was afraid to make a direct statement, as it might be wrong. The teacher saw me as defying her and decided quickly that she was not going to like me. She publicly humiliated me before the class for making mistakes until I was in tears. Even after the tears, I would have to stay after school and write, "I will pay attention to the teacher while in class" what seemed like hundreds of times on the black board: *I wlil pay atetenioth toe trechre whin calsl. I wlil pay atetenioth toe taechre whin calss. I wlil pay atetenioth toe taechre whin calss. I wlil pay atetenioth toe taechre whin calss. I wlil pay atetenioth toe taechre whin calss.*

The next morning as the students entered the classroom, they could see the black board full of misspelled words.There are no words to describe the humiliation I felt. I would become nauseated, my heart would race, and my face would flush. I had to hold back tears, which made my throat hurt from the strain. Because I was afraid of making a mistake, I would spend a lot of time trying to anticipate a mistake and how to cover it up. I began to daydream and withdraw emotionally to protect myself from the threat of being humiliated. I spent much of my time alone, climbing trees or taking solitary walks through the neighborhood. I would hide in the chest where all of our toys were kept in the corner of my closet or behind the clothes, hoping no one would see me cry.

That same year Mother found a reading tutor for me. I had to leave school at the appointed time and walk a few blocks to the tutor's home. My third-grade teacher would cause me to be late. If I got up at the correct time and left class, I got in trouble and again would be publicly humiliated before my fellow students, repeating the usual routine of staying after school to write hundreds of times on the blackboard whatever she wanted me to say. The words were always there in the morning for all the students to see.

I continued to find ways to hide my emotions from others and, hopefully, from myself. Crying to myself was a way for me to release my shame, but even crying was shameful for me. I believed crying only showed even more weakness. Therefore, I sought out a place of isolation to cry. This solitary place protected me emotionally from my fear of being disapproved of by others. I learned to show a stoic presence in order to hide my sadness. I could play with my classmates, cousins, or family like other children my age. However, I held in all the pain and agony of my shame, self-doubt, and loneliness.

One weekend when I was in the fourth grade, Mother went out of town. She normally left Martha, Chad and me in the care of our housekeeper, but this weekend it was Dad's turn to care for us. Dad's routine pattern of alcohol consumption had increased over the past several years and had begun to scare us, but this particular weekend was dramatically different. He came home from the farm already agitated and disoriented.

He began to rage against Chad, who was just acting like a normal four-year-old. Dad started screaming obscenities at us about whose children we were and continued yelling, "I wish that you had never been born. I will kill you." My brother started crying and ran to his room. Dad went to get his gun and then ran after him continuing to scream, "I will kill you."

Martha and I ran to save our brother. We gathered him up, ran to the bathroom, and locked the door. Dad found us and pounded on the door as he continued to shout. He kept yelling those obscenities, this time threatening to knock the door down as he shouted, "I will kill you all." The longer he yelled, the more enraged he became. We were all huddled in the bathroom, trembling with fear. We had never seen Dad this scary before, and we did not know what was going to happen. What if Dad did get the door down? What would happen to us? What if he shot through the door and hurt one of us? We had to get out of the house.

We tied sheets together and let ourselves down from the second story window. We ran for our *lives* to the neighbor's home. Chad did not stop crying until we were safe. When we returned home the next morning, Dad did not remember how he had acted the night before. When Mother returned from her trip we told her, but she indicated she thought we were making it up.

I was confused. What was happening to our family? Dad was becoming more violent towards us and especially his son. This is the same son, only a few years earlier, Dad had been so proud of when he was born. Mother pretended that a problem did not exist. The truth we had experienced was in sharp contrast to the words of a trusted parent, who said nothing believable happened.

Dad's drinking continued to increase. He took most of his rage out on Chad. I remember hearing Dad curse at Chad and say all kinds of degrading things. I remember when Dad attempted to kill Chad by holding him under the water while fishing. There happened to be some other fishermen who came by, saw what was happening, and stopped Dad from drowning Chad. I have memories of Dad holding a loaded gun, pointing it at Chad, and screaming that he wished that Chad had never been born. Mother would jump in between them to keep Dad from shooting. I remember Dad screaming at the top of his lungs in the grocery store at Martha that he wished that she had never been adopted. I felt so guilty that I could not stop his behavior. I was afraid that something would happen to Mother, Martha or Chad. I loved and hated my dad at the same time. His behavior scared me intensely when he was drinking. When he was sober, he was funny, and I thought he had a great deal of wisdom. Whenever I would go to him to talk to him—when he was sober—he would listen and give me counsel that I could understand.

Dad loved to fish. He would take me from time to time. We always had a good time. He would bait my hook and take off the line all the fish that I caught. I felt special on these trips. My fishing trip experiences were so different from the ones that Chad had. I yearned for more times when Dad was calm.

The summer after the fourth grade (1956–57), we were on our usual family vacation in the Colorado mountains. We rented a duplex so that Mother, Dad, and Chad were on one side and Martha and I were on the other side with Myrtle, the housekeeper, who always went with us. As a treat, Mother would give Martha and me fifty cents to go to the five and dime store to buy something. Martha would ask that I share one half of my money with her so she could save hers. I wanted my sister's approval so badly that I would let her have whatever I had or do almost anything she wanted so I could win her favor. She would return with all of her money still in her pocket. I would get into trouble each time for allowing this transaction. I was the person in the wrong for having a gullible heart. I do not remember Martha ever being reprimanded for being the manipulator.

That same summer, another incident influenced my understanding of my value and how my needs could be met. I liked to sleep on the screened-in porch of our rented cabin. It would get cold at night, so I would nestle down under the covers. Most times, I would pull the warm covers over my head and snuggle down toward the foot of the bed.

One night, I was awakened abruptly as Martha pulled me out of my warm sleeping position to reposition me at the head of the bed where it was cold. I told her to go away and leave me alone. She went back to her bed. I snuggled back down at the foot of the bed under the warm covers and went back to sleep. Then again, I was awakened as the result of her pulling me back out of the covers.

I shouted, "Leave me alone!" I was so angry with her for bothering with me. She proceeded to say that she needed me to be at the head of the bed. That was where I was supposed to sleep. Then she went back to her bed. By this time, I was so very angry that it took me awhile to calm down enough to rest. I hated being awakened in the middle of the night and especially being bothered. I hated being told what I ought to do by Martha when it was not my choice. It seemed like hours, but I was able finally to get back to sleep at the foot of my bed under the covers. To end it all, I was awakened a third time by her demanding that I sleep at the top of the bed and not under the covers at the foot of my bed.

I yelled, *"Leave me alone!"* and ran to wake Mother. My running into her room with Martha running behind me startled Mother. Martha sat quietly with a grin on her face while I frantically explained why I was there. I was talking so fast that I had to repeat myself a couple of times. In desperation, I asked Mother to tell Martha to stop waking me and to leave me alone. Mother just looked at me. I said it again—that I needed her to tell Martha not to wake me. Mother spoke directly to me and told me to go back to bed and Martha would not bother me any more. I did not trust that Martha would stop bothering me of her own choice. I was even more desperate, and I began to cry, pleading that she would specifically direct Martha to *"stop."* Mother said nothing.

I shouted, "I will scream until you tell Martha to quit bothering me!"

Mother just looked at me and then rolled over and pretended to be going back to sleep. How could she turn away from my need to have Martha leave me alone? I was powerless to do anything about keeping Martha away from me while I was sleeping. I did not even think of defending myself by hitting her, for I would have been blamed for it. I needed mother to protect me. I screamed the rest of the night, standing at the foot of my mother's bed. She played opossum but did nothing.

In fifth grade, (1957–58), after I had a long series of neurological and psychological tests, I was diagnosed with a learning disability called dyslexia. Finally, there was a name and maybe a solution. I was taken out of public school and sent to the only school in town that could help me learn to read. It was the school for the physically and mentally retarded (as it was called back in the late 1950s). That term "retarded" has had a long-lasting effect on my psyche.

On my first day to go to the new school, I was up early. I was ready and eager to learn to read. Then I would be like everyone else. I would blend in with my classmates and with my family and be accepted. I would get approval from everyone. No one would make fun of me any more. As I walked up the sidewalk to the entrance of the school, I found myself among students who labored with spastic paralysis as they walked and others who had a difficult time forming words to communicate. My soul screamed from within that I was not like these students. Oh . . . but wait! Perhaps I was like them and I had always been wrong about that too. Emotionally traumatized by the sight of the other students and my association with them, I was unable to learn anything. My hope and my dream of being normal melted away before my eyes. I slipped into believing at a very deep level that I was truly mentally retarded. I must be or why else would I be there at that school?

I continued to believe that I was damaged, and now with the experiences in the new school, I would never be any different. I had been created this way and there was no way to change the way I was formed. I felt I had no one to talk to about my feelings. No one took the initiative to talk to me about how my value as a person was separate from my special needs. My hope of reading and being able to fit in with the rest of my classmates shattered. This little lonely child cried in agony inside. To survive emotionally in public, I had to develop a strategy of denial, minimizing, covering up, blocking out, or disconnecting from the truth of my feelings. Hiding behind these defenses, allowed me to pretend that everything was all right. I could no longer pretend. My sense of shame overpowered me and I felt lost. The trauma of being in that school was more than I could handle.

I became so downcast that I became suicidal. As I stood with the bottle of aspirin in my hand alone in my bathroom, I contemplated taking a whole bottle of aspirin to end it all. I did not take the aspirin because I feared that if I failed I would be chastised for my actions. Being disapproved of and chastised for something was a far greater emotional burden than death would ever be. Ironically, it was a deep sense of failure that saved me that day. I never told anyone about my thought to end my life, and I was too lonely and embarrassed to ask for help. I was only ten and already carried a deep sense of shame and *isolation* from the world that overshadowed all of my feelings and thoughts. To cope, I cried alone. Words cannot describe the loneliness that I felt, for it went into my bones, into my heart and into my soul. What ten-year-old contemplates suicide? This was a very perilous place in my life.

Mother was aware that my mood had become withdrawn, and I began to carry my body in a bent-over manner from the weight of my burdens. We never discussed my feelings, but she saved me by putting me back in public school. It must have been hard for my mother to put me back in public school knowing that there would be no further help in teaching me how to read.

The following summer (1958), I had the opportunity to go to camp. I looked forward to it, as the summer can be so boring. Camp Waldemar offered many activities to do. I could "do" things successfully, and camp was the place to "do" things. Because I was home sick, I would write home often. Mother would send the letters back to me with the misspelled words *corrected.* I just knew that all the other campers could see these letters and the corrections. I felt like there was nothing that I could do to win her approval, and I feared the teasing by other campers.

No one at camp knew I could not read or spell as well as she could. I wanted a place where I could escape others knowing about these deep, dark secrets I hid. I was so humiliated. Martha was at camp with me. She did not get any letters sent back. I felt, and could justify by now from experience, that I was not loved as much as my sister. The camp term was six weeks long. I soon stopped writing letters to avoid repeated humiliation.

Dyslexia had not affected my coordination. I was limber and could do almost anything physically. I loved climbing trees, riding horses, ballet, jazz dancing, water skiing, roller skating, and tumbling on the trampoline. I had the courage to be in the recitals for ballet. I quit taking piano lessons as I was unable to get through the stage fright of knowing I had to perform in front of others. They would hear my every mistake. There was no way for me to hide from the sound of wrong notes as they filled the room.

I loved the outdoors. I would go fishing with my dad, play out on the farm, or walk in the woods. Competitive sports were out as I was emotionally unable to compete. My creative talents were expressed in my participation in the garden club for juniors where I won awards for my flower arrangements.

I had a special talent for putting things together. I was gifted with strong eye-hand coordination. The Christmas of my sixth-grade year (1958–59), my parents gave Chad a cardboard jail playhouse. Martha, now twelve, said that she could put it together. She was advanced beyond her age group in her ability to read, spell, and write. She got out all the pieces and laid them very carefully on the floor; then got out the instructions and proceeded to read them. I looked at the pieces, looked at the finished picture and took action to put it together long before my sister had finished reading the instructions. I could win approval for doing things or remembering details or directions from experience, but not from academics. There Martha excelled. She was a straight "A" student and never had to study very hard. I wasted so much time comparing myself to her. I was envious of her success.

Our family continued to attend the Episcopal Church, where I was taught all the Bible stories during Sunday school. I trusted with a child-like faith the truths found in those stories. I could identify, especially with Moses and Joseph, as they were born of one family and raised in another. I accepted that God had a plan for my life and that His intervention was part of that plan. I sang in the choir and, when I was big enough, I became an acolyte. When I was eleven, I attended Episcopal confirmation classes before making my public affirmation of faith and commitment to the responsibilities of my baptism and received the laying-on of hands by the Bishop. The laying-on of hands by the Bishop was for a special anointing of the gift of the Holy Spirit to "strengthen and empower" the person for service in the rest of his or her life. Confirmation in the Episcopal Church is when a baptized person, who has been instructed in the Christian faith, makes a mature, public affirmation of her faith.

In the spring of that same year, I stood before the congregation and said that I believed that Jesus Christ is the living Son of God. I accepted Him as my personal Lord and Savior and I pledged my commitment to follow Him in discipleship. This was a very special day for my family and for me.

Every year our Christmas tree stood with stately magnificence in the front entry hall where our spiraling staircase ascended gracefully to the opening at the second story balcony. When I was twelve, we had an especially tall and beautiful tree. We put all our lights and trimmings on it. We actually had to go to the attic and get down even the lights that we had not needed in previous years. As a family tradition, we did not take the tree down until New Years Day. This particular New Years Day (1960), the family had been at the tennis courts where everyone, except for me, played tennis. I sat watching the tennis ball go from side to side until I heard the sound of fire engines. I left the tennis courts and followed the sounds. I stopped when I found the fire trucks. A wood-frame home was raging out of control with flames.

People were screaming, "There is a baby inside. Someone, please help!"

I saw a mother with tears rolling down her face pleading for help as she yanked on the arm of one of the firefighters.

"Please help," she sobbed.

I saw the emergency and felt inadequate to help. My heart panicked for her. I wanted to stop her pain. It was so sad. People from all around the neighborhood gathered to watch the firefighters work to put out the fire and to find the baby. I hoped that the baby was alive and that the firefighters could save him. However, the fire was put out before that baby was found. The firefighters found the charred body of the baby amongst the rubble. I saw the mother being carried off by friends with her head buried in their arms, sobbing as though she would break.

I walked back to the tennis courts where the family was just finishing their games. I told Mother and Dad about what I had just seen. They agreed with me how sad it was for that family.

Once home, we went upstairs to get out of our tennis clothes. I was dressed first, so I started back down the stairs. I noticed a flicker in one of the light strands on the Christmas tree. It reminded me of the flame that appears when someone flicks his or her cigarette lighter. The flicker suddenly grew brighter.

I screamed for Dad, "The Christmas tree is on *fire!*"

Dad stepped into the hallway from his bedroom and saw the small flame. He grabbed a blanket off his bed and threw it on the tree. Mother stopped changing out of her tennis clothes to call the fire department. There was too much air under the blanked for it to smother the flame.

Dad asked me to go quickly downstairs and unplug the lights from under the tree before the flame got any bigger. I ran down the stairs, but by the time I got to the bottom, the tree was in full blaze.

I screamed, "I can't get under the tree to unplug the lights. I'm scared!"

This was a crisis, and I just ran out of the house. I sat on the curb, rocking back and forth and crying. I was terrified! I was afraid that Mother, Dad, and Chad would burn to death, as they could not get out. I believed that because I was too scared to get under the tree to unplug the lights, I had caused the fire to get bigger. I remembered the fire and the tragedy of the baby from that afternoon. I froze in fear out on that curb.

Then I saw the housekeeper come up the driveway in her car. I shouted to her that the house was on fire. She jumped out of her car leaving it to run into the flowerbeds before it stopped. She then ran inside toward the fire. I blamed myself for sending her into the fire and possibly causing her harm. I blamed myself for being out of control and screaming in fear.

Our house had two staircases. The grand circular one stood in the front hall and a second smaller and narrower one was hidden at the back of the home. To save their lungs and lives, the family crawled on the floor and down the back stairs to safety. Dad was able to get a garden hose and, with the housekeeper's help, extinguish the fire before the firefighters came. Even though the smoke damage was extensive, only the Christmas tree had caught fire. After he had put out the fire, Dad came and rescued me off the curb. He kept reassuring me that it was okay that I did not get under the tree to unplug the lights. Dad could be so understanding. I just kept *blaming* myself.

3

NOT ANOTHER DEFECT!

Halfway through my eighth-grade school year (1960–61), I began to complain of pain that went from the lower back through to the hip area and on down to the ankle. I had developed a physical problem of unknown origin, which influenced my ability to learn and added to my already struggling self-esteem. Because of all the different expressions of dance in which I was involved, my ballet teacher thought that I had pulled a muscle. I stopped tumbling on the trampoline, dancing jazz, which I dearly loved, and acrobatics, but not ballet. The pain continued. I stopped horseback riding and water skiing. I stopped climbing trees and hiking. The pain continued to intensify over time. My *disappointment* continued to increase as I was forced to let go of the things that I loved. Academically I was not gifted, but in the physical, I had a sense of accomplishment that had somewhat offset the failures in reading and school performance. Finally, I had to even stop my beloved ballet. I was becoming a blob of pain without anything that I could call "me."

The pain shifted from just being uncomfortable to keeping me awake at night. I would rock my entire body back and forth in the bed each night in order that I might get to sleep. This rocking helped to reduce the burning pain and the muscle cramps. Soon I was not able to walk without a limp due to the increased level of pain. I hurt sitting, walking, sleeping and generally all the time. The pain cramped, burned, throbbed, darted, tingled, and ached deeper than I could identify.

I had mentioned this pain to my mother a number of times. After several months, she became concerned, so she took me to the pediatrician. He agreed that I must have pulled a muscle, and rest from all activity was prescribed. However, the pain and the limp did not go away. I lost the natural rhythm of walking. My grades began to suffer, as I could not focus on anything except how badly I hurt or how sad I was in facing all the losses. I was overly self-conscious about the ever-intensifying limp and the differences in how each leg moved. I was confused and unable to identify where the confusion was coming from.

After a few more months (by this time six months of pain had gone by), the pediatrician sent me to an orthopedic surgeon, who, after an exam and several x-rays, diagnosed me as having a "slipped capitol femoral epiphysis" (damage to the bones in the hip socket).

Mother cried when she heard the diagnosis. That was only the second time that I had ever seen my mother cry. Years later, she told me she was so sorry. She felt responsible for the severity of deterioration and for the problems I was to face in the future. I was only thirteen and had no idea what path I would be walking down. Mother knew. She had to build a tough stance toward my physical recovery. At the time, I thought she did not care about or love me. I was basing that on an already established belief that I was not worthy of her love. Had she been overly protective or overly sympathetic to me, I would never have learned to walk or learned how to live with pain. God's grace gave my mother the ability to be strong in the face of both of us hurting. Mother could not see the emotional pain I experienced from a reading disability. She saw the mistakes. However, she could see the pain in my physical handicaps and responded to me with compassion and strength.

A slipped femoral epiphysis is an unusual, although not rare, disorder of the adolescent hip. For some reasons that are not well understood, the ball at the upper end of the femur (thigh bone) softens and slips off in a backward direction. A slip occurs because the growth plate between the epiphysis and the rest of the thigh bone cannot stand up to the stress place upon it. Most often, it develops during periods of accelerated growth, shortly after the onset of puberty. In most cases, the slipping of the epiphysis is a slow and gradual process. However, it may occur suddenly and be associated with a minor fall or trauma.

It occurs two to three times more often in males than in females. Early diagnosis provides the best chance to achieve the stabilization of the hip and reduction of future complications. The most common complications include the permanent alteration of blood supply to the femoral head (called avascular necrosis) and a loss of articular cartilage of the hip joint (referred to as chrondrolysis). Loss of articular cartilage may cause the hip to stiffen with permanent loss of motion, loss of ability of the joint to bend, shortening or shrinkage of a muscle or tendon and chronic pain.

Depending on the severity of deterioration of the epiphysis, surgery may be required in order that the surgeon can place pins in the hip to stabilize the socket. Three to four months or more depending on the severity of the destruction of the joint of non-weight bearing, may be required to ensure that the abnormal growth plate has fused. Placing pins through the socket to stabilize the joint has a side effect. The pins actually stop any further growth of the femur. The epiphysis of the femur is one of the growth joints for body height of the bones. With physical therapy, some range of motion can be gained. If the deterioration is minor, normal activities can be resumed. On a continuum, the more severe the destruction of the socket, the less range of motion can be regained and the less activity will be recommended. I had been diagnosed in the severe stage of deterioration.

I left the doctor's office on crutches so as not to put any weight on the leg until the bone had hardened. With today's modern medical advances, I might not have been required to be non-weight bearing for as long as I was, or maybe at all. Because of the significant degree of deterioration, I was advised to have surgery to place metal pins in the hip socket to prevent the epiphysis from slipping out any further.

A few weeks into the summer of 1960, the surgeon placed three long metal pins in the hip socket. The surgeon told me that because the pins were placed in the hip socket, there would be no more growth in my leg from hip to knee but that there would be from knee to ankle. It would be necessary for me to remain non-weight bearing until the bones had hardened again. Even though I was educated about this, I was unaware of how my body would *look* with one leg shorter than the other and how that would affect my self-esteem. I discovered that it was awkward to maneuver around on the crutches and it took some time to get used to using them with comfort. Fortunately, the school year had just ended and that gave me the summer to adjust to my new situation.

My self-esteem continued to suffer. I found it difficult to accept all the losses I was having to face and experience. I had lost the ability to do all the physical activities that I enjoyed. I lost my identity of being physically whole. I lost the affirmation associated with ballet. I lost my ability to focus on play or activities. I was consumed with pain emotionally and physically. I began to feel useless. *Doing* things had been my only way of developing some sense of self-esteem. I could not succeed in school. Now I was having my ability to get around to "do" things taken away from me. I was scared and felt uncertain about the future.

To help me find something to do from a sitting position, mother found a woman who would teach me to sew. In learning to sew, I discovered something new to do for which I had a natural talent. I saw where the pieces were to go. I did not need the pattern except for cutting the fabric. I soon moved away from bought patterns and began to design my own.

Dad suggested I take apart one of his suits to learn how to make finer garments. I began making everything from my own clothes to party dresses, and later, my husband's suits, my children's clothes, curtains and country quilts. I enjoyed the creativity of it, but I was not emotionally capable of believing how good I really was.

The junior high school I attended in the seventh and eighth grades was in a two-story building with no elevators. It was necessary for me to transfer to the other junior high because it was "handicapped accessible." By the time school started, I was tired of crutches. I had fallen down enough times to know that I was ready to ditch them. My hands had blisters on them, and my underarms were sore. I dropped things often. I never got use to the noise when something hit the floor.

Once school started, other students noticed my situation and asked questions that made my self-consciousness increase. Some students were concerned about how they could help, while others made fun of me. Because I was already supersensitive about criticism, I magnified the negative comments. When I became too tired for the crutches, I would switch to a wheel chair. It was easier to balance my schoolbooks and purse from a sitting position.

Mother had the shoe repairperson design a leg brace that went across my left shoulder and down to the right foot, holding it up and off the ground. When using crutches, this brace kept me from spontaneously putting weight on my leg. It was embarrassing to wear this brace. It went right between my breasts and distorted my blouse. Shoulder purses were not in style in my town. I was out of the mainstream in fashion. I was grateful I did not have to wear the brace when I was seated in the wheel chair.

All junior high school age children worry about what others think. I wanted and hated the attention I received. I wanted it because it helped me to feel valuable; I hated it because I feared others were either just pitying me or mocking me. I held my feelings about my situation quietly in my heart. I was embarrassed about being dyslexic and now about my physical disability. "Smile, and pretend that everything is under control." That was my family's motto.

I kept others away emotionally, as I pretended that everything was fine. If I talked about my true feelings, I would cry, and that would just add to the shame and embarrassment. I was so worried about what others saw. All the issues surrounding dyslexia, and now this silly brace, crutches and/or the wheelchair, just intensified how inadequate I felt. All the losses became one big disappointment to carry. (see Appendix A). I would get angry and sometimes sit at the top the stairs in our home and let my crutches plop one step at a time all the way down to the bottom. It sounded like I was falling down the stairs. Mother would come running and be really angry with me for scaring her. I was just plain mad that I had to be the way I was.

After seven months on crutches, the doctor said I was ready for the pins to be surgically removed (December 1961). I was on crutches one more month after recovering from the actual surgery. Then the surgeon said I could walk again (January 1962).

Great news! Walk again! No problem . . . right. I was not prepared for the pain to increase. I had been in pain for the last year. Even when I was non-weight bearing, the hip hurt. Like an arthritic joint, weather affected it. No medicine had been prescribed. I would complain, but no one else had any idea as to the degree of pain that I was feeling.

Once off the crutches, I walked with a terrible limp. My entire body dropped to one side as I put weight on the right leg. I pictured myself as walking like the Hunchback of Notre Dame. The muscles fatigued and cramped quickly. Pain continued, not only because of the bone but also because of the muscles. I did not know anything about pain management. All I could do is deny, cry, or fidget. It was too painful to sit still.

The leg was shorter than the other was. The shape of the leg was noticeably different in size. The leg had atrophied from non-use. The reality that the femur was not growing was now in stark clarity. I saw what the surgeon had told me would happen. I felt so deformed, twisted, misshapen, and visibly imperfect. This was just more than anyone should have to go through. I had to wear a 3/8 of an inch lift on my shoe. In addition, at age fourteen, I thought that *everyone* noticed. I had no range of motion. I would never again be able to do the activities I use to do. No running. Not even to the phone. No horseback riding. No carrying heavy packages. No springboard diving or any other high impact sport. No driving a car with standard transmission. No walking long distances because of the fatigue. This was *not* fair.

To keep my sanity, I found I needed to focus on what I could do because the list of losses was so long. I could swim, walk short distances, or sit for short periods of time. I was discovering that pain would remain with me for a lifetime. I feared I would always have a grotesque limp. There were so many fears I held inside. The bone would continue to deteriorate, which in the future would require additional surgeries. Because of the weight, I would only be able to have two pregnancies. I would not be allowed to even adopt a third child as carrying a third child would be too much weight on the hip.

I continued to rock myself to sleep at night to help with pain tolerance. The movement attracted my attention away from the pain. Who would want marry someone who moved around in the bed all night? Who would ever want to marry me with all these restrictions and problems?

Remaining thin would help me to postpone the inevitable future surgery. My life became focused on how I could preserve the hip that I had in order to delay any future surgeries for as long as I could. Maybe by the time I needed surgery, medicine would have developed something helpful.

My dad liked to hunt and shoot birds with the help of his bird dog, Charlie. For target practice, he used clay pigeons at the shooting range.

He kept his clay pigeons stored in boxes in our attic. This attic was the unfinished third floor of our home. The entrance to the attic staircase looked like just another closet in the upstairs hallway. I would disappear behind the door, closing it behind me, and ascend to my private sanctuary. I would often go up there when I was angry or sad and throw the clay pigeons with intense energy across the room, smashing them into the walls of the opposite side of the attic. I smashed and smashed until I no longer needed to. I would cry my heart out up there, praying to God the Father that He would have mercy on me, and make everything better.

Somehow, I did feel better, even though things did not change. I believed God is a loving father, a protector who would intervene on my behalf and had an overall plan for my life. In the quietness of the attic, I had long talks with God. In my child-like faith, I trusted him with my life and everything that was happening to me. I believed God had a meaning and a purpose for my life and all that I was going through. I just did not understand what that meaning was. I prayed for wisdom to understand, patience to wait and persistence to endure until my life was relieved of the emotional and physical pain. I knew He saw my heart. I guarded my heart from others out of fear of being hurt by them. Too many experiences had already proven to me this truth. I could not endure more pain.

I developed a fear of falling, as it might lead to me hurting myself. I had been bold in most physical activities that I used to do before hip surgery, so this fear was such a stranger to me. My friends were in the stage of "no fear." They were not leaving me out, but they went places I would not. Isolation was a common and familiar feeling for me.

Sadness and grief at the loss of my lifestyle weighed heavily on my shoulders. There were too many feelings all jumbled up in my heart and mind to form into words. The feeling that I had been made this way and that there was *no* way out of this situation overwhelmed me. When would it ever end? Now fourteen, I was developmentally more mature than at age ten. Because I had found a safe place to let out some of my frustrations, suicide was not an option any more. The blessings of the faith that had been born in my heart provided a relationship for me with God the Father, who sustained me. I had surrendered my trust to him because I believed He loved and cared for me. I felt confident He heard every conversation that we had. I did not feel inadequate when I talked with Him.

I believed that He loved me with all my flaws. I did not have to put my feelings into words. I just knew that He knew what I was trying to convey. I was also blessed with two very close friends who would listen to me and provide guidance. They would hold my brokenness in their confidence.

One of my special friends was Beth, who I considered my best childhood friend in the world. She lived across the street. It was to her home that I ran to the night Dad threatened to kill us all. We went almost everywhere together. When we could, we would dress alike. We would talk on the phone for hours. We shared our secrets, we laughed together, and we cried together. We rode our bicycles through the streets of town. We encouraged one another through love and honesty. She would go on our family vacations with us. I cherished our friendship.

The other of these special persons was my cousin, Luke. I did not know how to live with the pain, the altered life style, and the limitations I faced. I did not know how to cope with the uselessness or the embarrassment I felt. He was extremely popular and had been on the football team when his life was suddenly changed forever. Polio left him paralyzed from the waist down. I went to him for counsel. His love and compassion for me in itself was healing. We talked about the continued usefulness of ourselves even with our physical limitations. Luke encouraged me to embrace the pain, as it was a sign that I was alive. He suggested that I go out and do something for someone else when I hurt and that the pain would lessen or maybe even go away for a short time. He said that focusing on the pain and all of the losses, tended to increase the pain and uselessness. His wisdom proved to be true. I began to develop a life of giving to others in service. It was not easy. Doing something for others meant that I had to forget about myself. As I struggled with this new style of coping with the physical pain, I found it easy to accomplish. But in the emotional pain associated with the all the losses, I was not successful. The only way that I could cope with the emotional pain was to continue denying the truth that I was hurting or that I felt unworthy. My private self and my public self that others saw were becoming well defined and they were not necessarily congruent with one another.

Once off crutches, physical therapy was prescribed. Because of the limited range of motion, I had as the result of the damage and the inactivity for the last eight months, the physical therapist had her work cut out for her. Rehabilitating my muscles was a challenge. Everything was so tight. I had lost range of motion and the ability to move the leg with a smooth rhythm. In order to loosen the tightened muscles before exercises began, hot packs were placed on my hip for a while. Then the physical therapist and her assistant would stretch the leg. It hurt beyond my ability to tolerate the pain. I would either cry or get angry.

One day, filled with anger and self-pity, I planted my heels in resistance and refused to work. Because I was hurting and feeling sorry for myself, I kicked the therapist as she was trying to help me.

I will forever be grateful to that wise woman. She said, "Let me show you something, *dearie!*" She whizzed open the curtain that separated me from the next person, and there was a little four-year-old girl. She had been born without any hip sockets and had already had three surgeries to repair the sockets. The little girl was asked to get up and show me how well she could walk. She was so happy about life. Her face was animated, and she had the wonder of exploration in her eyes.

As I saw her struggle to walk even with her dramatic limp, I burst into tears. I found a deep sense of oneness with that little girl. I pleaded with God that I could have a sense of joy in my life. I saw that self-pity and anger were destroying me. God was faithful and the anger melted for a time.

I had a difficult time getting to my right foot. Putting on my socks was tricky. I was unable to get my foot to rest on the opposite knee. Therefore, I had to rest the foot on the seat of a chair and put the sock on from behind. It was almost impossible to clip my toenails. Then there was the struggle to put on pantyhose so that my heel was in the correct place. I eventually learned to adapt and successfully accomplish the tasks. I learned that if I put my right foot or leg into what ever I was putting on before my left then it was easier to get dressed.

Learning to walk again was hard work. I had to push through the pain and discomfort. Mother worked with me every day to help me with the home exercise program that the physical therapist designed. I could not do the exercises by myself and depended upon her help. I learned a heightened sense of self-discipline and persistence. The harder I worked, the more success I had. I learned to focus on the end result rather than the twisted physical image that I saw. For survival, I continued to deny that I actually hurt. I learned that if I focused on others and their needs, I did not have to face my pain and I would hurt less. I lost touch with the reality that I had needs, too. I projected my need for comfort onto helping others in their time of pain. I learned to minimize, if I could not deny, the degree of both physical and emotional pain. I learned to keep quiet about the degree of pain that I had because if I did not actually put it into words, then I did not have to face the reality of the degree of suffering that I was having on any particular day. I maintained a running dialogue with God, asking Him to bestow upon me the ability to endure. These conversations allowed me to remember that God had a plan for me. It helped me to stay focused on His promises and that He would deliver me from my trials. It sustained my belief that God loved me.

4

HIGH SCHOOL

Because of my academic struggles and my health situation during the eighth and ninth grades, my teachers advised that I repeat the ninth grade. I was mortified! What a blow to my self-esteem. I would not even be able to graduate with my classmates. I now faced another disappointment enveloped with public shame.

Dad came to the rescue to talk with me and to help me understand that I possibly could go away to school, thus postponing anyone knowing what grade I was actually in. He had gone to a military high school after he had graduated from high school thus repeating his last two years. His way of talking with me affirmed that I was acceptable as I was and that I was not a failure for repeating. That was the wonderful Dad of which I yearned to have more.

Sometimes Dad could talk with me, and sometimes, when he had difficulty talking, for example about dating, he would convey his concerns and love in other ways. One day he slipped an article from the daily newspaper under my bedroom door that he wanted me to read. It was about a woman who had been raped. Dad wrote on the top that she "was dressed in inappropriate clothes and was in a place she should not have gone." I believed that he was suggesting that if I dressed provocatively and went places that put me at risk that it would be my fault if I got into a sexual encounter that I had not planned. He was trying as best as he could to protect me from presenting my intentions and myself in a way that could ultimately harm me. I knew he was concerned for me and wanted me to be careful.

Mother and Dad were able to find a special high school for me to attend, but it was out of town. They made the sacrifice to allow me to be a border, returning home on holidays and in the summer. I was apprehensive about living away from home. I did not know what to expect in my new environment.

My academic salvation began when I went away (1962) to Hockaday, an all girls' school. I could postpone anyone knowing that I was repeating and I could attend a regular school. Hockaday was not like the other private school that I had attended when I was ten. Hockaday is a regular private school, one through twelfth grades that just happened to be in the beginning phase of a pilot program using the Gillingham method to teach dyslexic students to read.

I met daily with Mrs. Maxwell, my private tutor, three of the school years. My senior year, I met with Mrs. Woods daily to complete my training. The tutoring session was only one hour a day out of the regular school curriculum. I could disappear into her class and none of the other students were aware of where I had gone. I went unnoticed. What a joy that was. In her classroom, we repeated the same lessons over and over. I relearned all the letters and sounds of the alphabet. I wrote them in the air, wrote them on the blackboard, wrote them on a piece of notebook paper, closed my eyes, and wrote them as I pictured them. I said them out loud each time I drew them. I learned pronouns, verbs, prefixes and suffixes and whole words the same way I was learning phonics until it was second nature for me. In the tutor's room, it did not matter if I made a mistake. I knew she wanted to help me. I knew she believed in me. In addition, I believed that she knew I could learn to read. The high school blackboard experience became a healing ritual as I wrote words down. I was encouraged and affirmed for the times I successfully accomplished the correct spelling of the words. I was never embarrassed or humiliated for making a mistake.

The first year, I was not allowed to read for myself. I was read to, and all of my tests were oral. This gave my brain time to recapture the early stages of processing sounds and letters. Mother told me that when I reached eight months old, instead of practicing the crawling stage, I got up and began to walk. I missed out altogether on the co-ordination of the brain's information between hemispheres.

By the end of the first year, I was allowed to read for myself again. Glenda, another boarding student, agreed to read to me all of my lessons aloud. Most of the tests in the high school were essay in form. The year I was not allowed to read, I was also not allowed to take written tests in any subject. Either I knew the answers or I did not. There is no way to try to finesse the answer when I had to take the test orally. Once I was able to read and write for myself, I felt like there was more hope for actually succeeding and I was able to take the written tests. Each essay test was evaluated on content and grammar. I usually would get an A in content and an F in grammar. My grammar grades improved each year, and by the twelfth grade, I was passing.

Algebra and geometry were no problem. I excelled to the point I was allowed to teach the geometry classes when the teacher was away. I always made an A in math. I ran into difficulty in math when the problem was in written word form. Strangely, I am less likely to transpose numbers, unless anxious, than letters. I was a natural at geometry. I saw three-dimensionally very easily.

It was a requirement to take a foreign language before graduation. I flunked French and Spanish. I could not hear the words, see the letters appropriately or pronounce back what I was hearing. Latin was the last choice. Latin was not a conversational language and therefore relieved some of the stress. I just had to memorize new vocabulary words, spell them correctly, and only occasionally say them out loud. We spent most of the class time translating the Latin into English. This process was actually possible for me to accomplish and to earn a passing grade. Since so many of the English words are from Latin roots, I actually learned English far better than I would have imagined. My English grades went up, and I began to make C's instead of the usual D.

The teachers in school were encouraging and believed that I was capable of succeeding. They would give me positive feedback on a regular basis. My self-esteem began to bloom as I began to find ways to perform with academic success. I made A's in math; B's in history, science, and Latin; and C's in English.

I won an award for being named one of the favorite boarding students all four years of high school—an award that is given to students who exemplify leadership and moral character as defined by the founder of the school. I was elected to be President of my class in the boarding department in tenth grade. I was elected to be President of the House Council my senior year. The House Council was to the boarding department as the Student Council was to the public school. To my amazement, many students looked up to me as a leader. This was different from my earlier years. I had been called *retard,* and not many people wanted to be seen as the friend of a retard. There were other students at Hockaday who had dyslexia, and we were all treated with respect and encouragement. I developed friendships while there that have lasted a lifetime.

Barbie, one of the girls in my group, had an adult friend whose name was Dee, who was her mother away from home. Dee adopted our entire group. She provided counsel, wisdom, and encouragement. She invited us to stay overnight in her home many times over the four years. Barbie, Becky, Margaret, Charla, Carolyn, and I would stay up late at night giggling and telling all kinds of stories. Dee was our home-away-from-home and our mother figure. I needed the time and the affirmation that Dee had to give. She was my example of what I had missed from my own mother. Dee helped rebuild the foundation for me to believe in myself that I had lost so many years before.

Hockaday's gym had an Olympic-size swimming pool. I was allowed to swim laps every school day for four years. I had my daily reading tutor and my daily swim. I had specific daily land exercises to do. The swimming along with the exercises helped me to keep the muscles strong and to reduce the pain. Continuing to live in chronic pain challenged my ability to define myself as normal. But I was beginning to have more hope about life.

My self-esteem was growing due to the academic successes and the affirmation of classmates. However, living in pain, combined with how I saw my body image, continued to influence how I protected myself. Since I experienced some level of pain all the time, I chose to keep silent about my discomfort. I learned very quickly that people got tired of hearing me always talk about how much I hurt. The weather, too much physical exercise, and unresolved emotions all increased the level of pain. I continued to minimize, deny, and disconnect from the pain and the emotions that surfaced. I continued to emotionally withdraw from people at large. I would find a quiet isolated space when I was hurting. I had learned all of those same skills as I learned to cope with having dyslexia. These were my survival skills, which allowed me the ability to function in every day life.

I pretended I did not hurt, and sometimes I succeeded in hiding the truth from others. Nevertheless, my close friends could see right through my pretense. For my public side I maintain a smile and say that everything was fine. Inside, I might be in agony.

As my self-esteem improved, I wanted to risk dating. I was willing to risk allowing someone to get close to my heart. I still had so many questions that remained about living with eternal pain, limited range of motion and changed lifestyle. How would I cope? What are the consequences of taking medications to reduce the pain over a long period? What about complications? How many surgeries would be in my future? How many scars from the surgeries would mar my body more? Who would choose me for marriage with so many restrictions from the beginning? I could only have a limited number of children. I felt reasonably sure that there would be someone who would be happy with a family of four. However, the "but" did gnaw at me from time to time. Would I be able to develop a physically intimate relationship that would be satisfying to my husband as well as me? Would it hurt my hip? As a young teen, that was something that experience had not yet taught me.

I was not able to attend Sunday school as a border. We were, however, able to attend the worship service. I had memorized the Episcopal Liturgy, which could be repeated whenever I needed to for encouragement or even as a prayer. I read scripture and prayed daily to find strength to keep going. I continued my intimate running dialogue with God, expressing my feelings about life and asking for His grace to endure. I was confident in His faithfulness.

I was confident that, in time, the pains in my life would be resolved. I claimed many of Paul's sayings from the New Testament as sources of strength, which helped me to make some sense of my struggles. My favorite was "We have the mind of Christ" (1 Corinthians 2:16, RSV). That helped me regroup and clear the emotional confusion.

I was learning to focus on my new skills, which seemed to allow the dyslexia symptoms to be at rest. However, when anxious, stressed or fatigued, the symptoms would surface. When feeling sadness, pain, discouragement, embarrassment, loneliness, or anxiousness, the following scriptures brought me strength:

> "We know that in everything God works for good with those who love him, who are called according to his purpose. For those whom he foreknew he also predestined to be conformed to the image of his son, in order that he might be the first-born among many. And those whom he predestined he also called; and those whom he called he also justified; and those whom he justified he also glorified." (Romans 8:28–30, RSV)
>
> "I can do all things in him who strengthens me" (Philippians 4:13, RSV).

My mother would encourage me by stating that character was developed through hardships. She kept telling me I was becoming strong in nature and steadfast in courage. I accepted this life, for I wanted the strength of character; however, I did not want to hurt. Character is a major part of who I am as an individual. It is how I do what I do. It is why I do the things that I do.

> "Suffering produces endurance, and endurance produces character, and character produces hope, and hope does not disappoint us, because God's love has been poured into our hearts through the Holy Spirit which is given to us." (Romans 5:3–5, RSV)
>
> "Many are the afflictions of the righteous, but the Lord delivers him out of them all." (Psalm 34:19, RSV)

It is through suffering that I learn who I really am. However, there must be something that is present within me, which enables me to push through the hardships without becoming and remaining bitter. Do I really know who I am until I face a hardship? If life is easy and goes along the way that I want it to, have I laid a foundation in my character that prepares me for success or losses? How do I resolve being wounded by others, or even our hurting others? What responsibility to myself and to others do I have to face my true self and be transformed? What was transformation going to look like? I really had no idea. I just believed that God promised to transform me into the image of His son someday, somehow.

It is written that the Apostle Paul had a thorn in the flesh. I imagined it was a similar hip problem or even dyslexia. Paul had asked three times for his affliction to be removed, but God left it for a greater good. I could relate. My faith was steadfast in that God would also bring my suffering to a greater good. God the Father was the ultimate father I did not have. I loved my earthly father, but many times his words and his actions hurt me. God the Father never hurt me. He never abandoned me. I believe He never asked me to do more than the two of us could do together. He was the planner and creator of my life. He had formed me in my mother's womb and then had placed me in a family to provide the care and the resources I needed. He was intimately involved in what happened to me because He loved me. He answered prayers. He could see my heart. I yearned to know more about Him. My faith was actually the glue that held me together and gave me a sense of identity. I had a reason for why all the pain had happened. I had a source of strength to pull from when I had nothing left. I had a reason to believe in life.

I enjoyed reading the bible. I also enjoyed reading the writings of Kahlil Gibran. I could get lost in the mystery in his written words. Because I was raised with music in the home, it was natural for me to listen to Classical music when my nerves were stressed. Classical music brought to me into a peaceful space. The dormitory was noisy, and the music was a balm to the ears. I loved art, and I could lose time looking at works by the masters. I loved to visit the museums to see the paintings of the old masters. I yearned to have the masters" ability to express my emotions as they could.

With the help of academic achievement, the strengthening of my muscles, which actually reduced the visible limp, and the development of good friends, I was beginning to come out of the hole I felt I had fallen into. I was able to begin to look for value in myself that I had not discovered before. I was beginning to entertain the idea that I just might be of value to myself and to someone else. How I saw myself and how I felt about my achievements were changing.

The day of graduation (1966) was a monumental, emotional high for my family and for me. My cousin Adam was there and cried for joy. He had always been a loyal supporter of me and I had not known it. I had succeeded in hurdling the reading disability. I had begun to trust my judgments. I had begun to believe in my intelligence. I had developed wisdom about life. I had matured in my faith and my understanding of God. I had learned that, with my persistent efforts and Gods help, all things could be accomplished.

I was accepted into Endicott Junior College where I could specialize in fashion design. I had begun to believe I had talent, and I would have the opportunity to use my skills there without all the other superfluous academic classes. I had designed and sewn many of my own clothes. I had designed and made dresses for my close friends as graduation presents. I had designed and made a formal dress, which I wore in a debutante pageant my junior year.

Most of the classes that I took in junior college were art related. Fashion Design was like playing paper dolls again. We created little patterns and made them in the fabric of choice. To my surprise, I sailed through academically. One day in my drawing class, we were to present our drawings to the class. When it was my turn, the professor took my sketch, with a charcoal stick drew a line down the middle, and held it up for the class. His explanation was that the right side had form and the left side did, too, but the picture as a whole was out of proportion. He proceeded to explain to the class that I had dyslexia and my brain worked in conflict with itself. One of my eyes saw the left side of things and the other the right side. As a whole picture, the drawing was unbalanced. He asked the class to look closely so they would not forget what a drawing would look like by someone who had dyslexia. If the professor wanted to teach on dyslexia, he could have referred to drawings by Leonardo da Vinci, who also has been reported to be dyslexic, not to me!

I was beyond mortified. Where did he get that knowledge? Had he deliberately looked in the students' files to find something that he could use to humiliate me? I had thought, and had hoped, all that was behind me. I wanted to scream at the top of my lungs long enough to let out all the rage and the humiliation that welled up in my heart. Instead, I was able to hold it together until the class was over.

I did not take the negative critique as I had in the past, with silence. I went directly to the Dean and stated my case. At the next class, the professor apologized to me. The Dean had required the professor to give me a passing grade without requiring me to finish the semester. I was almost glad that had happened. I was able to realize I was developing boundaries appropriate to guard my self-esteem.

5

TWO BLIND DATES

During the summers of high school and into college, we would have spectacular parties in our home. There were a number of popular local bands and we would book them to come and play. Martha and I could plan the menu with endless amounts of food. Mother's only requirement was that she was particular about who she wanted us to invite.

We would make the list of her "acceptable" girls and guys. Then I would have to pair them together. So many of my friends were involved in steady relationships. That was against Mother's rules—no going steady with just one young man. It was awkward for some of my friends because their boyfriend or girlfriend may not be on Mother's approved list. Couples were put together and invited to the party that way. If the young man did not want to bring the girl listed on the invitation, he could decline to come to the party. Getting past that strangeness, the parties were always a big success.

Mother wanted us to date many different kinds of men. If we dated just one young man, she believed we would not be able to make an informed choice regarding a marriage partner. I did sneak behind her back while I was away at school and had one steady boyfriend. As we matured, we realized the value of dating others. We dated for over two years before we decided to stop dating each other. While at home in the summers, I honored her request to date a variety of young men. My friends were helpful by setting me up with blind dates during the summers.

The summer between my freshman and sophomore years in college, I was asked to go on a blind date with a friend of a co-worker from my summer job. The plan was to go in separate cars and all meet for dinner.

After he picked me up, he said he had forgotten something at his apartment and he needed to go back to get it before we met the other couple at the restaurant. He invited me into the apartment while he went to get what he had forgotten. I should have waited in the hot car, but because my friend had known him and had recommended him, I assumed that he was a safe date.

At first, he treated me as though I was a pretty young woman. I did not sense that my limp bothered him. I did not feel inadequate or shy. I felt confident and in control of my life. After a few minutes in the apartment, he forced himself on me. It happened so fast that I could not defend myself. All I could think of was that it was my fault, as I should not have gone into the apartment. I did not even think about screaming or clawing my way to freedom. I felt victimized and unable to take charge to bring about a different outcome.

I kept saying, "Stop," but it had no effect. He just became more forceful, holding me down with his hands and legs. Sexually, it hurt, and I was forced to be in positions that were compromising to my hip. My leg was in excruciating pain and I felt like it was being ripped out of my hip socket. The time seemed to stand still. I did not think the pain would ever end. I began sobbing and pleaded with him to stop, but he just kept on until he was finished.

When it was all over, he told me to get up, clean up, and we would go to dinner. I was shocked that he was so nonchalant about the devastating event that had just happened to me. I was bruised, bleeding, shamed, and disoriented beyond my ability to process.

Like a robot, I did what he said and attempted to clean up. However, my body felt so dirty. The world was swirling around me, and I was not sure that I was going to be able to stand. I felt sick to my stomach. My mouth began to gush with saliva, and I was not sure I could get to the bathroom quickly enough before throwing up. After emptying the contents of my stomach, I was overcome with tears. My tears kept pouring out, and just about the time I thought that I had control, the tears started falling again. My make-up was all over my face and my hair was a mess. I struggled to find any coping skill that would allow me to "act as if it had not happened." I had gone into his apartment of my free choice, but I did not ask for sexual intimacy. I had not been flirtatious, nor was I dressed in a loose fashion. What happened?

My old coping skills slowly began to assist me so that I could minimize, deny, and disconnect from the pain. I think that I really was more in shock and therefore numb, rather than being successful with faking it. I was so traumatized that I went to dinner as planned. I did not even think of getting a cab and going right home. During dinner, I was miserable sitting next to the man who had just raped me. My friend noticed that something was wrong with me and asked about it. I was too full of shame to admit to her what had happened. I was too ashamed to talk about it. I was able to ask the friend to take me home after dinner.

I stuffed the guilt and dirtiness I felt. Before the rape, I had begun to repair my self-esteem. Through education, physical therapy, and some successes, I began to accept that I had some value. Because of this sense of worth, I was able to challenge the college professor who humiliated me in front of the art class. However, all of this crumbled as the result of the rape. The agony of shame returned as I wondered if I was responsible for the entire experience.

A few months after the rape experience, a high school classmate asked me to go on a blind date with one of her long time friends who was on leave from the army. Why I went I do not know. Maybe it was because I had known my friend for a long time or because I felt motivated not to allow myself to be put in that same situation ever again. Maybe I needed to reestablish control over my life. I now knew to be on the watch for sexual advances.

I was rather apprehensive as I saw his car drive up to the curb. Just as he opened the car door to step out, the skies opened up and let loose of a sea of water. He ran for the front door. He was drenched nonetheless. When I opened the front door to meet David, he was sopping wet. The water was dripping off his eyelids and running down his face. He looked at me with the silliest expression, and he had a sense of humility about his being wet. I looked into those big blue eyes, and I fell head over heels for him.

A dozen red roses came from him the next day with a note that read, "I enjoyed our time together. When can we have another date?"

David and I dated for several months, getting to know one another with comfort and compatibility. He had had polio as a child, and he had encountered his own struggles on his way back to health. I felt we understood each other. It seemed that David accepted me with all of my limitations. He was funny and outgoing. He had energy about life that I enjoyed being around. I became spellbound in love with him, and I daydreamed about spending the rest of my life with him. I know I fell in love with him with a passion as big as the state of Texas.

As his family began to feel comfortable around me, they shared more and more about their family life. His mother, Sarah, shared her agonies in having a child with polio and the paralysis her son faced. She had worked very hard in their home exercise program to enable him to walk again. As she described how she put hot packs on his legs before all the stretching exercises, I remembered my own rehabilitation in learning to walk again. I felt at home with his family. Sarah also shared how wonderful the doctor had been through her son's illness. She stated that the doctor was the same one who had delivered both of her sons.

When Sarah called the doctor by name, something in the memory banks of my mind rang a loud bell. She was talking about the husband of my first-grade teacher! When I said to her that I thought that his wife had been my first-grade teacher, Sarah said his wife had gone back to teaching a few months after the doctor's premature death. No wonder my teacher had such difficulty with me. Her skills were rusty and she was grieving her losses. My scars were not completely healed, but this knowledge did give me an understanding into the fact that I was not the problem. Her losses and her ability to process her losses were.

How strange that I would date someone from another town close to mine whose pediatrician was the wife of my first-grade teacher!

Because I felt confident in our relationship, I decided to risk sharing my date rape experience with David. I had a sense that if I did not tell him, I would be founding our relationship on "withheld information," and the strength of a solid marriage lay in open communication. My family origin had too many secrets to be a healthy family. I had also used the camouflage of silence to protect my emotions. I felt it was time to risk developing this new relationship on truth and openness.

I had not told anyone, and it was a huge risk for me to be telling it at all. As I shared the story with him, it was as if I was experiencing the date rape all over again. I was sick at my stomach and my hands were sweaty. My heart was racing, which led to a mild form of hyperventilation. My mouth became dry. I felt like my throat was going to close before I could share the experience.

I told him how I had felt violated. I described the lingering guilt. I explained how I did not believe that I had asked for the sexual encounter. I felt that I had tried to stop it but that he had been stronger than I was. I talked about the shame I carried in my heart and how dirty I felt. I was at the point of tears from reliving the story as I told it to him. He could see I was in excruciating agony. In a heartfelt response, he put his hand on my shoulder to comfort me. I finished and waited. The wait seemed so long. After he heard my story, he turned his head away from me and was silent for a long while.

Then David said, "I forgive you."

6

THE LIGHT OF LIFE

David and I married in 1968 on Easter Sunday, just shy of a year after the date rape. I stood at the altar in the Episcopal church and promised before God, friends and family to stay married for better or worse until "death do us part." This was a serious commitment of my heart. I planned to live happily ever after.

A few months after we were married, David received orders to report for duty in Vietnam. He was already in the military stationed at Fort Hood. The year was stressful for both of us.

I spent most of the year that David and I were apart with my parents. I noticed that I was beginning to develop a new ability to talk with my parents. Dad had been in World War II and he had the words I needed to hear. I began to understand many of the issues that they faced as a couple. My eyes were opened as I began to know my parents for who they were as people separate from their role as parents.

David returned safely from Vietnam and we started our marriage all over again. I took my role as a wife seriously. I really did not have extensive experience in relationship building. I thought that I was supposed to put my needs aside to care for him. I noticed there was something different after his return in the quality of our relationship. I could not put my finger on it at the time. It seemed that he was overprotective of me. I sensed that he was not listening to me talk to him anymore. I did not understand what was happening and he would not talk about it.

One month after he returned, we were talking about some more of the fears I had developed from having dyslexia. He told me that he felt I was over exaggerating the situation and that I just needed to get over it. My feelings were hurt and, feeling emotionally unsafe, I shut down. I was in the second most intimate relationship in my life (following that of my parents), and I felt that my reality was not being validated. I was not emotionally mature enough to challenge his response, and I reverted to my old behavior patterns of emotional isolation. I decided I had been mistaken about being able to share openly with him. I thought that he had been empathetic before we married. Had I been blind in love? Did he change? I gave only a portion of my life to him from that day forward. I was in conflict because I loved him deeply and now was disappointed. How could I hold these two opposite feelings at the same time? Love was stronger so I stuffed the disappointment. I set out to learn how to be a wife and to honor David as I had promised. We were married two and a half years when Andrew, our first child, arrived (1970). He was so cute! We wanted another child as soon as I was healthy enough to become pregnant again.

My second pregnancy had complications. The doctor suggested bed rest lasting about six months due to my threatening to miscarry. Ruth arrived eight weeks premature weighing only four and one-half pounds (1972). The first seventy-two hours were a crisis for all of us. The pediatrician was not sure Ruth would survive. I did not know if I could face the loss of her death. I cried buckets. Fortunately, the only complication she experienced was that she lost weight. She needed to stay in the hospital for a month to gain strength and to regain the weight that she had lost. The day I brought her home was a day to be celebrated. I took all of my clothes out of one of my dresser drawers and used it for her baby bed. She was too small for her bed. I cut pampers in half to fit her. I bought doll clothes, as there were no clothes for premature babies in the stores. Because of the trauma of her first few weeks, I feel I probably have over protected her during the course of her life.

Soon after her birth, I developed complications from having endometriosis, which the doctor said would require a hysterectomy to correct. I knew that I was not supposed to have any more children. However, the fact that now my body physically could not, rather than my decision not to, presented an unexpected adjustment for me.

When I woke from surgery, my mother-in-law was standing over me saying that I must be a sinner; otherwise, God would not be punishing me with the need to have had a hysterectomy. I was aghast that Sarah would say such a thing, much less believe it. The God I loved would never have punished me this way. I believed my health was the result of all the extra x-rays from the hip and not punishment. I was discussing with David his mother's words and my belief in God, to which his response was, "Well, *you* did have sex as a teenager. I have read that early sex causes endometriosis to develop." I had no idea to what medical study he was referring.

I could only think that he referring to the date rape. I did not know what was in his mind. I did not ask, as I did not want to know the answer. If he had held an attitude of disgust for me all those years because I had been raped, I did not want to know. It would mean that I would have to process it with him, and I was scared of what he might say. So, I said nothing. I buried it as far down into my subconscious as I could.

After I returned home from the hospital, one of my next-door neighbors asked me, "So, how does it feel to be an it?" What a strange question. I was most certainly not an "it." I am a female; but now, what did it mean to be a woman? Was it just the ability to have children? What was feminine? Was womanhood just a role that had been given to me by society or cultural norms? How was it different from masculinity? Was my role to be married and have babies? Was my "place" to work in the home? However, they are only roles. Was there a different way for me to find the answer?

The surgery left me feeling like a dirty, worn out dishrag. I had no energy and I did not feel feminine. I decided to have reconstructive plastic surgery to boost my self-esteem and maybe help me to find an identity in womanhood. I had lost so much weight that I resembled an adolescent boy. I was looking for the answers to my femininity questions outside of myself.

Breast implant surgery was a success. I was sexy with very shapely curves. I began to have attention that I had never experienced before. People came out of the woodwork to talk to me. Gradually it began to dawn on me that the attention was purely physical. The attention was not because someone wanted to know my heart. They were just flirting. I looked in the mirror one day and decided to have the breast implants taken out. The doctor was confused and attempted to talk me out of that decision. I yearned for people to love me for who I was—not what I had or what I looked like. I was searching for a femininity that lasts over time no matter what shape my body had. I defined my femininity as beauty within. It is the kind of beauty that does not wash off at the end of the day.

Within three months after the hysterectomy, the endometriosis had begun to grow back. This is not happening to me! My heart sank to the pit of my stomach. I was so disappointed. I could not cope with another surgery so soon; therefore the doctor put me on hormones in an attempt to shrink the infection. The medicine did keep the endometriosis from getting larger. I reached my limit in being able to tolerate the extra hormones. One day I was slamming cabinet doors, throwing things around the room and yelling at everyone. The children were crying because they thought I was angry with them. David did not know what to do as he watched me, so he called the doctor. The doctor took me off the medicine at the risk of the endometriosis returning. The cost of my sanity outweighed the possibility of another future surgery.

Mother and Dad had begun to visit our home frequently. It warmed my heart to see them in the role of grandparent. I was able to observe them reaching out to my children with love. I was able to imagine how they had done the same with me, even though I was unable to feel it.

Within the year following female surgery, my hip socket had finally deteriorated to the point a hip replacement was necessary. Tolerating the increased pain took most of my energy just to exist. My duties as a new mother and wife were being compromised. David's job took him off shore a week at a time, leaving me with the responsibility of our children. They were so young—Andrew three and Ruth one and a half—and I was almost a basket case with pain. It was out of the question for me to take pain pills, as they made me sleepy.

The doctor prescribed an anti-inflammatory, which worked in the beginning, but I soon built up a tolerance even to the strongest dose I could take. I sought consultation with three prestigious doctors at three different well-known clinics across the country. I got three different opinions as to how their method of surgery would repair my hip. I chose the one that had the quickest recovery.

I went to Houston, Texas and had a total hip replacement (1974). The type of hip replacement I chose involved gluing the new hardware to my body. I would be able to walk within a few days post surgery. The other procedures involved metal screws to bracket in the hardware and possibly bone grafts. With this procedure, I would be non-weight bearing from six weeks to three months.

With the hardware glued in, the hip was strong enough to walk on immediately after surgery. My sister and her husband were gracious to invite me into their home in Houston for three weeks while I recovered. I had been advised to stay in the Houston area near the doctor. There had been cases in which the new hip implants had been rejected by the patient's body. These incidents were rare but the doctor wanted to take all precautions. Recovery was fast. The pain was almost gone. The horrible limp was almost nonexistent. For the first time in thirteen years, I was almost pain-free. The only limitation was that I could not perform impact sport activities.

Freedom! The legs were the same length. I threw away all of my shoes, because they had lifts built into them, and got new cute ones. I actually was able to wear sandals or walk barefooted. I could run toward my toddlers to save them if they went too close to the street. I could run for the phone. I had unlimited range of motion. Freedom, gratitude, and joy were overwhelming emotions. It is so difficult to explain this new emotional high. I was now *normal.* I did not have the sense that I was physically retarded anymore. It was a miracle. The transitions I experienced as I learned to adapt to accepting all my losses had been such a struggle. The liberation was now breathtaking.

Even though I could have so many new possibilities in a new lifestyle, I chose to go on with my activities as before. I did add hiking and nature walks, but chose carefully, as this new hip had, at the time of surgery, only been proven for a thirteen-year life span. I wanted to preserve it for as long as I could. Revisions, I was told, might not be as successful. I was twenty-seven, and at thirteen-year intervals, I could have up to four or five more replacements in my lifetime.

Three months after recovering from hip surgery, David's job relocated him to Houston. A year later, a tumor was discovered in my body. As I was going through the tests to determine what it was, no doctor could assure me that it was not cancer. The doctor suspected endometriosis had grown back, but there was no guarantee that was true. Fear chilled my soul. I was just learning how to live free of pain. Why now? I felt it so unfair to have to stop again. If it were cancer, I might have pain again, have to face more loss or even die. Who would raise my children? If David remarried, would this step-mom love my children? Oh God, please do not let this be cancer. My life was just beginning to be full again. I had only just begun to feel *normal*. Why do I have to stop and endure another mishap? This is not fair! I have had enough!

I did not want to die. I was so scared I could not focus on the details of life. I was emotionally fighting off panic feelings that rushed over me, coming from out of nowhere. I found my emotions inside shaking like a seizure. Tears were an alternative to fright. Believing that everything was in God's hands was very difficult. This was a real crisis in my faith journey. For the first time in my life of faith, I began to question and I began to doubt.

Waiting for surgery, and then the pathology report, seemed like an eternity. I had plenty of time to worry about the possible outcome. I actually made myself sick worrying about what was going to happen regardless of whether I worried or not. I was greatly relieved that the tumor was benign (1976). However, questions haunted me: Was the faith that I had leaned on and that which had sustained me a "Truth?" Would it sustain me beyond the grave? Was there an eternity? What had I done in my life worthy of showing to God? I had spent my life hiding the gifts and talent that He had given to me. I had denied that I was lovable. I had shied away from His leadings so many times. Would He forgive me?

I became an avid reader searching for something that would bring peace. Wayne Muller in his audiotape, *Touching the Divine* defines spiritual work most poignantly. He states, "There are times in all of our lives when we are forced to reach deep into ourselves to feel the truth or our real nature. For each of us there comes a moment when we can no longer live our lives by accident." He continues by stating "life throws us into questions that some of us refuse to ask until we are confronted by death or dome tragedy in our lives." I could relate. He continued with more questions: "What do I know to be most deeply true? What do I love? Who do I believe myself to be? What have I place on the center of the altar of my life? What will people find in the ashes of my incarnation when this is over? How shall I live my life knowing that I will die and what is my gift to the family of earth?" These were the same questions I was asking. He concluded by saying that "these questions come around and around like a spiral going ever deeper into the meaning of life." (Muller, 1994).

After listening to his audiotape, I entered into serious reflection, prayer, reading, and discussions with people who might know and help me find the answers. I was not given an answer; I was asked a question that actually became the answer. I began to hear a call to give up my choices for my life. The calling got louder "to throw my life away and become an empty vessel for God to fill." A living death was the call I heard. Now wait a minute. I feared death from cancer, but to consciously choose to die was a very different and very strange request.

The concept of giving up reminded me of all the times in my past when life's events or other people had dominated my soul. I resisted with all that was in me to retain control. I really did not know what my life was, but it was all that was familiar. Even in all its pain and disappointments, the life I knew was less frightening than change. I was terrified of the unknown and the possibility of having to accept more sorrow in the new path. Jesus' example was of loneliness, being misunderstood, betrayed, hardships, pain, suffering, and being abandoned by friends and God. I was tired of hurting physically and emotionally. His path also included love, commitment, selflessness, denial of self for the benefit of others, and total forgiveness. Jesus knew who He was, and He used His talents to the fulfillment of God. I did not see myself as any of those. I had buried my talents with fear and excuses, finding ways to avoid putting myself in positions to be ridiculed. I had built a magnificent wall to protect myself from emotional vulnerability. I had learned how to present one public side of myself and guard the internal side in secret. I felt so *unworthy* to respond to His calling.

My search ended in the middle of the night when I was awakened from a sound sleep by what felt like a bolt of lightning crashing into my chest. My body went into convulsions, shaking uncontrollably. Once awake, I heard a loud sound of the wind blowing violently. My first thought was the coming of the Holy Spirit at Pentecost. Was this God? The very same God of the entire universe? Was He right there in my bedroom? I felt an incredible fearful awe. I was not afraid of harm or destruction. I was, in a sense, in a state of holy reverence for the omnipotence and majesty of

God. Who was I that He would come to have a personal meeting with me? My heart was racing so fast that my veins felt as though they were going to explode. I second-guessed the experience by saying to myself that maybe I was having a heart attack, and what I heard was only the blood rushing through my veins. I was beyond terrified. I thought if I hid under the covers, I would discover I was dreaming. In truth, there is nowhere I could go to hide from God. I accepted the invitation to converse with God. I accepted the truth there was nowhere I could hide and He would not come and find me. I accepted that His choice of me was because it was His choice and there was nothing I had or would ever do to deserve His presence.

Then I heard His loud, yet gentle voice calling me again to give up my life and to follow Him. He was calling me to set aside my will for His. He was calling upon me to give up self-desire, self-decisions, and self-direction. He was calling me to put aside my definition of myself and to be transformed by Him. He was calling me into death. I was so afraid of the unknown. I curled into a fetal position my face down into my chest in the bed and squinted my eyes tightly shut.

Something mysterious happened. I found my eyes were open and I was no longer in the bed. I was somewhere else. I was standing in the middle of an empty landscape. It was void of anything familiar except a top (sky), light gray in color, and a bottom (land), a little darker gray. I became even more aware as I realized God had always chosen me and He would hound me until I chose Him.

His question again, "Will you come and *follow* me?"

I panicked as I looked for a way to surrender to His invitation. I remembered that Jesus would by my guide, for he had gone before and knew the way. I yelled "Jesus" and stretched out my hand into the unknown, asking Him to show me the way. At the instant I felt my hand touch the hand of Jesus everything became a brilliant, pure white radiating light. Pulsating from the center of the white light, were rays of pure colors—red, blue, green, yellow, purple, orange—all of them. The brightness of the light did not hide its essence, for it was the risen Christ.

I knew without words being spoken that it was He. I felt as though I had been gone from my home for a very long time and now I was back where I belonged with Christ. He emitted from that brilliant white light total acceptance and a pure holy love for me. I felt peace words cannot explain. I felt comfort. I felt connection. I felt embraced by a love that was indescribable. I felt secure. I was content. I was satisfied.

Our conversation was not dependent upon words. He conveyed that His sacrifice was necessary and sufficient. His life and death on earth flashed through my consciousness. It was like someone showing a video and reading the story simultaneously at the same instant. Time did not exist. Past, present and future were the same. Messages and insights were conveyed without words. I just knew. He is who He says He is! He will protect me. He would always go before me, showing me the way to live. His love for me was more comforting than snuggling in front of a fireplace. More peaceful than anything I have ever experienced. More beautiful than the most gorgeous of all sunsets. As real and yet as mysterious as the feel of the wind blowing across my face. Words seem to really take away from the wonder and depth of the encounter. Nevertheless, words are all that I have to try to describe the mysterious.

The next thing I knew, I was back in my own bedroom, sitting in an upright position on the edge of my bed. It took a few minutes for me to actually realize I was awake and back in my bedroom. I no longer heard the rushing of the wind or felt as if my blood was racing violently through my veins. Slowly I could sense I was still filled with wonder and amazement.

Where had I gone? Had I actually died and gone to Heaven? I felt as though I had and had been resurrected. I was empty, and yet full. Empowered, yet humble. I was aware that I am a small speck in the universe, and yet infinitely important to God. I was awed that there is another place other than this earth. I was surprised by the feeling that I had a sense I had returned home after being away for a long time. That must mean I had been there before and I knew it as home even if it were only in that I was in the mind of God before I was created. I was with God even then. I rested in peace through the rest of the night. So much to process.

I did not tell anyone, as I was concerned I might be called psychotic. Another concern was that people would think I had made it up. The visitation was too awesome to be devalued as being made up. In addition, some of my neighbors believed that visions were of the devil. I did not want to share this beautiful experience with them. They would just make fun of it. It was my present from God, and I held it in secret. I was not well-versed in the scriptures and could not quote verses with them to support my experience. In fact, I could not even prove that the vision was real.

The next day Martha came to visit me. She kept asking what new make-up I had bought. She said that I had an unusual glow about my face. She said I really looked at peace, and she thought maybe I had had a face lift. Her witness was what I needed to verify that my experience with the Holy one was more than a dream. I have never again seen such a brilliant, white light or felt so peaceful. Over the course of the rest of my life, my understanding of this experience and my relationship with God would change many times as it grew deeper and wider.

As time passed, I began to grieve having to be back here in this world. Like the disciples Peter and John, I wanted to pitch my tent on the mountaintop and live there forever. I longed to go back to wherever *it* was. I yearned to be with Jesus again. I no longer felt I fit here on earth. I had been enlightened and all of the rest of life was boring, cruel and more struggles. Soon, I began to understand that I was called to let go of all the old garbage and to replace it with truth and honest, open expressions about who I am. I was called to search my motives. I was called to be in alignment with the person that God originally had in mind when He formed me in my mother's womb.

I had built so many walls to protect me, and now I was called to be vulnerable. I had made many choices based on what I wanted or what I was trying to avoid. Now He was calling me to hear only His voice and to respond. I was apprehensive. I had never walked this path before.

I found I was remembering people and places I had not thought of in a long time. I remembered the cousin, Luke, who had been such an inspiration to me when I was a teenager. I remembered that I had never told him how much his counsel had inspired me. I decided to call Luke and tell him. I got his phone number from my mother, but found that I could not call him. My throat would close and I would begin to cry every time I contemplated making the call. So to relieve my stress and follow God's leading, I attempted to write a letter. I judged my words as insufficient and never sent any of the many letters that I had written.

A few weeks into this gentle nudging by the Holy Spirit, Mother called and invited us to come for the weekend. I gathered the kids, and off we went. After we got there, Mother told me that Luke was at his ranch (his second home), just a few miles from her home, also for that same weekend. He had asked for all of us to come for dinner.

I knew that God, in His grace, was giving me another chance. I had been so concerned with how I would be perceived that I could not follow God's leading. However, there I was again, and His insistence was obvious. I prayed for courage and grace to verbally tell Luke at dinner. I prayed for an opportunity for us to be alone so that I would have time to speak from my heart. During the evening, God was faithful and did provide several opportunities for me to speak. Each time my throat would tighten, and I would feel that if I spoke, I would not stop crying. I was experiencing an overwhelming sense of gratitude and love for Luke, and I could not say those words. The evening ended and I had not been faithful to God nor honored the life of my cousin.

The following Monday, Mother called and said that Luke died early that morning. I felt so empty. God knew Luke needed to hear what I had to say. My brother did call Luke the night before he died. Chad had the same nudging and he had followed his calling. How could I understand my disobedience and all of my excuses? There was no undoing what I had done. How many times had I neglected to follow God's nudging because of all the petty reasons that I made up? How often had I not trusted that if God has called me to a task, He would give me the courage and resources to accomplish it? Listening to God and then following His instruction is a major part of walking in the friendship that He offers me. I found forgiveness but not till I had searched my soul and accepted responsibility for my fear.

The next bit of house-cleaning was that God turned me toward my marriage. Those walls that I had built for emotional protection needed to come down. I began to talk with David about myself, my needs in the marriage and that I really was lonely. I began to tell him that I did not feel a union with him. I admitted I felt that our communication was less than satisfying. I shared I did not feel that he was listening to me. It had seemed to me that he always had something other than what I was saying on his mind. I wanted to talk about the changes in our relationship that had occurred after his tour in Vietnam. I wanted to talk about how we differed in child-rearing. I wanted to talk about how different we were becoming. I was honest about the dryness of our marriage and how I wanted either for things to change or for a divorce.

We began marriage therapy. There was just enough time to get the issues out in the open, and then David was offered a new job in West Texas (1980). We began our life out west with nothing resolved. We had not had time to process our differences or the opportunity to find resolution.

7

WHY HAS GOD FORSAKEN ME?

Life is kind when it gives us brief periods of rest before another hurdle to climb. Spiritually, the first year we moved to West Texas was good. It was on the heels of a life of hope, almost pain free and with a renewed faith. Little did I know I would be led into the darkest night of my soul, barely to come out alive. I really do mean *alive.*

All of our unresolved issues resurfaced with bold clarity. My coping skills were not sufficient to help me deal with what was ahead of me. My acceptance of my calling from God was about to be tested by fire and purified.

After David and I married, we both left our roots and became Presbyterian. We believed that it was important to raise our children in one faith. I was active in our new local church teaching Sunday school. I was one of the presenters in a four-state regional workshop. I later was nominated to serve as a Deacon on the church's governing board.

My commitment to serve grew more easily than my ability to grow spiritually or psychologically. I was fearful of changing inside. It required that I change in my ability to communicate my deep wishes. I prayed all the time for help and guidance. I made a special attempt to hear the voice of God and respond. I vacillated between the courage to respond to God's leadings and resisting out of fear or lack of trust.

One day I heard Him ask me to go to a church and tell a special woman a special message from Him. Her face, a picture of the church, and the message flashed before me. I thought that, if I really go and do this, others would think me really bizarre. I had not met this woman.

After the nudging from God became stronger and I could no longer push Him away, I left the house to do what He was sending me to do. I drove around town and did not see the church.

"Great! I got out of this," I thought as I started home.

I got out of that embarrassment. But, lo and behold, on the way home, there was the church. I circled the block many times before I got the courage to park. After I parked, I sat in the car reassuring myself that God had sent me to do His work. I got out of the car and went into the church. As I entered the church building, a woman asked me why I was there and if could she help me.

I told her I had no idea why I was there. She told me I might find the answer in the sanctuary and pointed the way. I followed her instruction and found the sanctuary. Feeling like a complete fool, I knelt to pray. After praying, I got up to leave. But exiting from the room just across from the sanctuary walked the woman to whom I was supposed to give God's loving message. Tears rolling down her face, she walked toward me. I explained how I got there to the church and the message I was to give her was that God heard her prayers and would honor them. He would bless her ministry. She had been praying with her prayer group for hours asking for answers to her prayers. She invited me to enter her prayer group. This group became a help to me in the days ahead.

Because we had just moved to a new town, I had not had time to develop trusting friendships. Even though I had been asked to join her prayer group, I felt isolated. I was ashamed to admit I needed help. I was scared and unable to talk to my husband, so I returned to holding everything inside. David's new job had begun to take most of his attention away from the marriage and his time with our children. It seemed he had become more impatient with the children and critical of me. He would scream at them with words I felt were damaging to their self-esteems. I remembered all the hurtful words that had been said to me, and I hurt doubly. I withered under my own memories of childhood, and I was unable to emotionally protect my own children from the same things that hurt me. His focus was his new job, how he was perceived, how he needed to change to fit in, the duties, and the new people. Partying was also required as part of the social atmosphere.

The company parties with their indiscriminate drinking, the fake conversation, climbing the social ladder, and getting sitters for the children so we could attend those parties and company vacations all repulsed me. My husband needed these social interactions for his progression in his new career. I felt devalued and my needs rejected. Had I been in a different place in my life, I would have known that this was not a rejection of me. I would also have been able to verbalize my feelings and needs as a wife and mother. So many people might not have been ultimately hurt by my choices and actions. However, I was not in that other place. I was angry, alone and in agony. I felt abandoned.

The emotional pain level once again reached an equal magnitude to that of my bone problems. My body could not distinguish between physical and emotional pains. Both took on physical manifestations. To some degree, I had been able to talk about the physical pain, but the emotional pain was not acceptable to have or to express. I learned these response patterns not only for my own survival, but also from my parents.

To numb the pain, I began to drink. David was drinking, so I justified my drinking by thinking I would be able to hide what I drank. But, something happened to me. I became a closet drunk. I drank until I was emotionally numb or passed out. Very quickly, I found myself trapped. I could not stop. David and I began to argue, and we said so many hurtful words. It would have been kinder if I had been able to say what I had wanted to say to him in a sober state, even if those sober words hurt. But the drunken words cut like knives into both of our hearts.

Our children were caught in the middle. David taught them to be caretakers of their sick mother. My own family dynamics were mimicking that of my upbringing. I swore I would not do to my children what had happened to me, but there I was, doing it. The imposed role of caretaking would haunt them for many years to come. It would destroy many of their own relationships into adulthood.

I grew up hating my father's drinking behaviors. I hated the fear I lived in, never knowing when he would become a monster. I hated watching him become verbally cruel and hurtful to my brother. I feared for Chad as he drove to bars late in the night looking for Dad to bring him safely home. I hated the embarrassment I felt when we were in public and Dad was drunk or verbally ugly due to his irritability. Moreover, I hated the changes in his otherwise wonderful personality. He was sometimes so funny and witty. He had incredible insight into people. I loved him deeply, and I think that is why my emotions were so intense. I was disappointed by love. I was angry with Mother for not protecting me.

Mother was a stoic and held everything in. Dad was hysterical when drinking. Mother's response to him was cold, and she shut him out from herself emotionally and physically. His addiction was never discussed with us. We did not know when we were young that Dad was an alcoholic. Silence about family situations is not always best. It would have been healthy for Mother to tell us that the problem belonged to Dad and that we did not own the problem. Martha, Chad and I carried the blame for Dad's behavior and felt personally responsible. We needed to be set free from this inappropriate responsibility. We experienced the effects of his addiction in mood swings and somtimes scary behaviors. I found myself hating me for becoming just like that which I hated in my father. To my horror, I found that my personality was changing, too. I swore I would never be like him, and there I was, becoming just like him. It seemed so strange that the thing that I hated most, I became. Fortunately, it was that same hate that brought me out of my addictions. It gave me the motivation to struggle through therapy and eventually to become and remain sober.

I began the search for sobriety. I went to a psychiatrist, but he said I was still playing games and that I really was not ready to be sober. His response was difficult for me to process. I had gone to him for help and I remained confused as to why and how he came to that conclusion. I tried on my own to resist the temptation to drink. I remember many times being curled up in a fetal position in the corner of our bedroom, rocking back and forth, pleading with God for help. Many times a black ghost-like figure would manifest itself in front of me like a mirage. It seemed to have more power over me and I would eventually give in to drinking again.

My love for my family and my inability to stop drinking on my own power, plus desperation, led me to seek admission to a rehabilitation center. In that facility, I went through detoxification and an Alcoholics Anonymous twelve-step program, only to return home to the same problems. I saw the problem as a relationship problem because I thought it was rooted in my marriage. I knew there were things my husband needed to change. David saw my drinking problem as belonging solely to me. I had not yet developed the emotional maturity to understand I had the right to my feelings, opinions, and choices. I did not have to change to please others, and I did not have to feel guilty that I felt the way I did. I had not developed the verbal skills to express in a constructive way my needs. David refused to go to therapy with me; he thought it was my problem alone and therefore, his presence in the therapy room was not needed. I needed the situation to change, but it was not changing. I needed his help. I was so angry.

I went back to drinking. This led me to choose another rehabilitation center. As I look back now, I believe I was waiting for David to change, and therefore it would be easier for me to change. I was giving to him a responsibility that was not his and I set myself up for failure.

The second rehab center focused on the roots of my drinking and the behavior changes necessary to live a sober lifestyle. What was I running from? What was the pain? How was I projecting my problems onto others and holding them responsible for my lack of decisions or resolutions? It really was a painful journey to go within to face my monsters. I would get sick to my stomach as the memories surfaced and I looked them squarely in the face. I cried and cried buckets from a place that was deeper than I knew existed as I grieved for all the hurt that I had experienced and all the hurt I had inflicted on others. I was able to verbalize, probably for the first time in my life, the sorrow I carried. I had learned to stuff my feelings, as I felt they further showed my weaknesses and because I needed to be in control. This was a beginning for me to tell my story for the first time.

Looking into the truth that I had avoided was really painful. I was facing accountability in a sharp way. On one particular day in therapy, the issues were getting too deep. I was fearful of facing the truth. I got up to run for the door to escape the pain.

The therapist said in a loud voice, "Go ahead and run. That is how you have handled everything in the past. Go ahead and *run!*"

I stood with my back to the therapist and with my hand on the doorknob, ready to make my escape. I began to scream at the top of my lungs and shake the doorknob violently. I knew that if I did run out the door, I would never be sober. Even though my emotions were screaming, my will held my hand frozen securely on the doorknob.

I choose not to run out the door. I returned to the chair and, with fear and trembling, I faced the issue of how and by whom my boundaries had been violated. The boundary I am referring to here is my own identity. I was able to express my wounds from dyslexia. I was able to put into words how I saw myself with my limp and twisted body image. I was able to describe the negative criticism I had felt from my mother growing up. I was able to put into words my hatred for my dad's drinking behaviors. I was able to express my feeling of being unwanted by my birth mother. After much delving into my parents and my relationship with them, I was able to discover that they did the best they could and I actually admitted that I loved them deeply.

I explored the losses associated with the lifestyle required because of my physical disability. The idea of "abandonment" and the emotions and behaviors associated with being adopted first became known in this time of therapy. I came to understand that I believed there was something wrong with me; otherwise, I would not have been given up for adoption. I came to understand that these beliefs were false. I became aware of how false beliefs were only a distortion of my reality. I was ready to rewrite my belief system. This was the first time I had ever written down on paper my life story. Once I was able to write the details down and to tell my therapist the events of my life, I felt I would be sober forever.

Feeling "well," I returned home with determination to remain sober. I started to go to AA for continuing healing and support. However, when I went to my first meeting, I saw too many people I knew. Pride sent me right out the back door. I realized quickly that not all of the buried issues were in fact healed. I had only touched the surface. I had only identified some of the issues, but the lasting transformation that the change within required had not yet been formed.

Although I tried, I was unable to stop drinking using sheer will. Why could my own will not sustain me? Sheer will was the way I had pushed through dyslexia. My will coupled with persistence taught me to push through the physical pain and learn to walk again. With all the might in me, I could not find the strength to overcome my desire to drink. The roots were deeper than I could imagine. Without those roots being uprooted, exposed, and healed, I was soon back into my old habits. I spiraled down into an even darker place. I felt that I was experiencing hell right here on earth.

The world became black and barren. I felt so isolated. I became empty of anything positive. I began to curse and blame my birth mother for conceiving me. I began to curse the environment in which I grew up. In addition, I began to curse God for abandoning me when I was crying out so desperately for healing. This was the first time in my life I had felt that God was not answering my prayers. I was experiencing my own personal "Job" story. I was full of rage that I was alive. I became consumed with fury that I was not able to be in control of the situation. I blamed my dad for the environment in which I grew up. I blamed him for teaching me the coping skill of drinking. I blamed God for abandoning me. Christ had come in the past but He was now nowhere to be found. Was I being left to suffer? This difficult place full of rage carried such an emotional intensity that it was about to consume my very life; and then, the very healing that I needed was born out of this very dark place.

I began to search for my roots, mainly because I wanted to blame someone besides myself for my becoming an alcoholic. Just by chance, the mother of a friend of my daughter's had been reunited with her birth mother. I called this birth mother and asked her how she had found her daughter. With her direction, I began to look for my birth mother.

Every step of the way, I faced squarely the fear of rejection, the fear that my needs would be denied or that I might find something that, because it was more painful than I had ever experienced, I would not be able to cope with. I was surprised to discover the fear of rejection carried such a powerful influence over my choices and behaviors. I had no idea how it had guided my emotional responses to life situations. I was able to see that I had strong emotional responses to not having my needs met. I felt fear but did not understand the magnitude at that time. I experienced only that fear as related to being adopted.

The first action that I took was to write the judge in the county who had issued my final adoption decree and asked that my records be opened. I said my reasons were because I was looking for medical information that might be genetic. For example: did my birth mother have dyslexia, bone problems, cancer, high blood pressure, or something else?

The county clerk called me and said the judge did not grant that kind of request, but she would hand carry my letter to him and ask on my behalf. It was a wonderful surprise to open a letter from her and find a copy of my final adoption decree tucked neatly inside. I was again surprised by the document's contents. On the form were the names of my birth mother, Kate, and birth father, Steve. I discovered the name she had given to me at my birth was also on the document. Who was this other person recorded on the legal document? This new name presented yet another crisis to my identity. Who am I? I did not even like the original name. I was bonded to my name of Jeanne. This other name was foreign and intrusive into my life. Yet, it represented the first seven months of life in a different world. What had been those experiences?

Next, I wrote the county in which I was born and asked for a birth certificate using my original name, Donna. I was issued a new certificate. This should have been a sealed document, but for some reason, I was sent a copy. I contacted the chamber of commerce in the town where I was born, according to the new birth certificae, under the pretense of completing a genealogical trace and asked for information about where the old newspapers were kept. The woman on the phone asked who I was looking for and I told her I was looking for Kate McCoy.

She stated, "I knew her. She used to have a blue-eyed baby girl with the prettiest brown curly hair. I wonder what ever happened to that baby. If you find out, please let me know."

My throat closed up, and I could not speak. I wanted to shout, *"That's me!"* but an overwhelming fear bound my throat closed. As suddenly as my throat closed, it opened, and I was able to say, "That is me. I am looking for Kate." She told me she knew where some of Kate's family members lived and she would call them to ask about Kate's whereabouts. She stated she also had an adopted daughter. She continued by stating she was trying to help her daughter locate her birth mother. She understood what I was going through. I believe she answered the phone that day as a blessing from heaven.

When she called back, she told me Kate had died a few years before but some of the relatives were willing to talk to me. She apologized for having to tell me the disappointing news and wished me well in the continuation of my search to find other family members.

I wept. I was so sad. Why had the search ended with me finding my birth mother but not being able to talk to her? I had so many questions that now will never be answered. All the doors to find Kate had opened miraculously, as though the information was suppose to find its way to me. Yet, it led to a dead end. Why did it have to turn out this way? My need to talk to Kate could not ever be met. There was an empty space where I needed her to be. As I experienced that empty place, I became aware that I had always restlessly searched for a way to fill it.

After I had some time to sort through these emotions, I called the relatives, Seth and Roda. They told me I had an older half-sister, Nancy, who had also been given up for adoption, two younger half-sisters, Karen and Susanna, and two younger half-brothers, Pete and Mark. The relatives knew where Nancy lived and gave me her number. They did not know where the other siblings lived.

I called Nancy. It is so strange to call a perfect stranger and announce that I was her sister. Bless Nancy; she took it in stride. I went to her home to meet her, and discovered that we are very much alike. She is gifted in playing the piano and in singing. She loves to sew and loves nature and traveling. She shared her open adoption story with me. She described her visiting Kate several times throughout her life. She described the other siblings, for she had also met them. When I had talked on the phone to the relatives, they had told me that Kate's doctor delivered me at her home. Nancy knew the house where our birth mother had lived, so she took me there. The home looked like it had been abandoned for many years. We were able to dislodge the warped screen door open, and we went in. Only a few minutes inside, I was overcome by a heavy weight of sadness, and all I could do is fall to my knees and weep. I missed something. I could not identify what I was missing as an actual person or event. It was an indefinable sense of grief for something deep within my heart.

After we walked out the front door, I stood on the front porch for a brief moment looking out into the front yard. The view of the dry barren ground and the few struggling trees and feeling the gentle breeze triggered a memory. I remembered one of my repeating dreams. In that dream, I would be standing on a front porch. The porch would be made of wood that was worn and discolored from the weather. The yard would be barren and dry. There were three trees in the yard: two trees to the left and one to the right of the well, worn pathway leading away from the home. In the dream, I could feel the wind and hear the whistling sound as the wind moves. The dream carried with the visual images the feelings of emptiness and aloneness. Behold, as I stood on the front porch, I felt as though I was actually standing in that scene of my dream. Had it only been a dream? Was it only a co-incidence that where I was resembled a memory? Or perhaps was it a real memory that had been stored in the memory banks of my very early infancy? I probably will never know.

Nancy then took me to visit with Seth and Roda and later we went to visit with two of Kate's long time friends, Abbie and Rachel. Through them, I found out the situation that led to my adoption and something about Kate's character. She had carried an overwhelming sense of shame for an untimely pregnancy. Her society and her community's fundamental religion had been verbally judgmental and cruel. Not only was she shamed, but also, the baby that she was carrying was shamed (it had to be hidden from the world). I have not been able to find out much about my birth father, Steven, as the information about him has not been forthcoming. This remains a mystery to me, which I pray will one day be revealed.

I came away from the visit with more information than I knew what to do with. Kate was creative, talented, left-handed, witty, and strong willed. She loved to swim and loved to play volleyball. She did not like school and therefore was often absent. Her mother had abandoned her when she was around ten. She and her older sister, Claudia, went to live with a relative so that her father, Philip, could continue working. In that home, she became heavily influenced by her Aunt Ada's strict religious belief system. I was told that Kate was taught that only shameful girls got pregnant out of marriage. In her late teens, she married and moved away. She returned with her first child several years later after becoming separated from her husband. She had to work to support herself and her child. When Kate discovered that she was pregnant with me, she faced a crisis. Socially and religiously, she faced shame from her community. Her job, because it was serving the public, would not allow her to work and be pregnant. Her friends, Abbie and Rachel, told me in order to keep her job while pregnant, Kate bound her stomach to give the appearance of being slim. They also told me Kate had attempted to abort the pregnancy. Abbie and Rachel had always wondered "if I was alright because I had been so squeezed up inside and all that."

In spite of her shame leading to her attempts to use a home remedy to abort the pregnancy, God had a plan for my life. I believe it was by His grace that I am alive to share this story. I am grateful Kate failed to abort me. I am grateful to have life. Even with all the struggles my life has given to me, I am alive. Life is a gift from God.

I grieve for Kate when I imagine how it must have been for her to have been so judged by her relatives and the abusive religious system that was the predominant faith in that particular town. As I have carried my own sense of shame, I could relate to her carrying hers. Was I also carrying Kate's shame and it really was not mine to carry? I was seven months old when adopted. What memories and emotions were given to me to carry in that short time? I was told once I was born, Kate loved me. It was the untimely pregnancy she had not wanted. For emotional and financial reasons, she chose to place me for adoption. I can only imagine the grief she felt. Her friends told me she grieved for me for the rest of her life.

After seven more months of searching, I found my other siblings. When I went to visit them all except for Mark, they had made banners which they had strung out all over their apartment complex, welcoming me to their homes. I was filled with tears and gratitude for all of their love. By getting to know Susanna, Karen, and Pete, I found very special friends. Like Nancy, they are like me is so many ways. Through them, I have come to know Kate in a special way. I have come to know me. I was given the gift of connection to my roots.

Seth and Roda told me that my biological grandmother, Leah, was full-blooded Native American. They thought that I might be Cherokee, Chickasaw, or Choctaw but they could not remember for sure. I have not been able to find documentation to prove which tribe. Through Leah's lineage, I am a descendant of the Native American peoples.

It seemed natural for me, at this point, to talk to my mother about my search for my biological roots. At first, she was uncertain as to why I had chosen to search. Once she understood my need to know and my need to find my roots, she went to her office and pulled out of her filing cabinet the social history that the social worker had given to her many years before. She had stored it in a special place to give to me when I was ready. The detailed document filled in all the other details that I had not been able to gather from conversations with Kate's family members. The document did give me information about my birth father, but not where I could find him. That is still a mystery.

I was awed by all the people who helped me along the adoption search, by those who accepted me; and, my mother for her gift of the documents that she had held in secret. I was blessed because others were willing to share their stories with me. A part of my identity had been missing and with their help, I was able to put more pieces of my life together.

Who are the Cherokee, Chickasaw, and Choctaw? My fascination with them sent me to read as much as I could find about Native American history and traditions. The more I read the more pride was born in my heart. Somewhere along the way, I read about the possible medical link to alcoholism. I was convinced I had read that Native Americans have a higher percentage of alcoholism than other groups. I cannot remember any one article that actually stated a specific reference to alcoholism being the result of a genetic factor; however, I was certain that I had read it: therefore, I assumed I had inherited the gene. This personal belief had a powerful effect on my ability to feel empowered to make any changes. In spite of what I found and the courage in the journey to find my roots, I felt doomed to be trapped in the cycle of alcoholism. Without hope, I descended quickly into an even deeper, darker place.

8

AN AWAKENING

The discomfort and pain intensified to a critical level beyond my ability to cope with or to tolerate. Running away to stop the pain was a familiar pattern. One afternoon after drinking heavily, I told the children that I would be back; I got in my car, and without any thought other than how badly I was hurting and how badly I needed to get away from the pain, I ran away. I was not consciously choosing to abandon my children, but they later told me they felt that I had. I did not stop to hold on to the doorknob this time as I had done several years before while in the therapist's office. Because I had been drinking heavily, I did not get too far down the road before I passed out at the wheel. My car went into an open field, tearing down the owner's fence. The car continued until it hit a tree head-on. My head jerked forward and hit the steering wheel, which broke my glasses. My left eye was bloodshot from the force of impact. I had bruises all over, and my chest and my head were sore. The police officer who found me took me to jail and put me in a cell to sleep it off. I was not taken to the hospital to be evaluated for a concussion. The cruelty of my behavior will live with me for the rest of my life. I had not told my children I was leaving the house, and I did not call my husband to let him know where I was. My family had to worry in agony all night regarding my safety. They suffered because of my brokenness and anger. They suffered because I did not seek to resolve the unresolved issues I brought into marriage and motherhood.

In the middle of the night, a person dressed in a uniform came into the cell and held me down while he tore off my underpants and then raped me. I struggled to get away, but I was too weak from the trauma of the accident to stop him. My body was already bruised, and my head hurt from the concussion. He was stronger than I was. My mouth was covered by his nasty hand and I could not scream. I would have thought I was dreaming except for the pain of it all. After he finished with me, he left me in agony all alone in the cell. I felt like garbage that had been thrown out and left to rot, full of maggots, and any other vile thing that comes to mind. I felt like I had deserved to be treated the way that I had been.

God, where are you? Why have you abandoned me? Why have I been raped again?

I pleaded in prayer but no one answered. Maybe God did not care anymore. Maybe I had stepped across the line of His wanting to be part of my life. I was so empty. Self blame coupled with shame overshadowed my ability to believe God actually still loved me. How could I file charges against some one that I could not even identify? I had been arrested for drunken driving, so who would believe me? Who would believe that the rape had occurred while I was in the jail cell?

Adding to the pain of the accident and to the rape experience was the emotional pain of feeling utterly and completely abandoned by my friend, God. Alone and in deep agony, time seemed to stand still. Tears from my heart poured and poured out from the depth of my soul. I felt sick to my stomach. I was uncertain if the nausea was from too much alcohol, the trauma of the accident or the rape. I hurt too badly to throw up, so I tried to lie as still as I could. In the solemn quietness of the night, God did come and He did answer.

Out of nowhere, I saw Christ standing in front of the opening to a cave. The long white flowing tunic that He wore was gently blowing in a breeze, His arms outstretched with his nail scarred palms open. He said to me in a gentle compassionate voice, "My sacrifice saved you not only in and for eternity, but also to live the life that you were created to live right *now* on this earth. I saved you this day to *live.* Satan has played havoc for a time, but that is now over." He assured me that the hell I believed I had experienced on earth was nothing compared to the hell of eternity. Was I dreaming or was it real? I did not know which. I do know that the experience and the message made a profound impression on me.

Emotionally beaten but grateful that I had not hurt or killed anyone in my drunken driving, I called a friend the next morning and asked her to call my husband. They came together to get me. I needed Barbara, my friend and prayer partner, to be with David when he came to get me, as I feared his wrath. My husband had the right to be angry. I had been so cruel to him. I had made him suffer all night wondering where I might be. I had remained addicted. I had not stopped drinking.

This addiction was so powerful and greater than my ability to "win" sobriety on my own. My best efforts had failed. The two rehabilitation centers and the continued therapy were slow in helping me to change. Many issues were necessary to face. Change had a cost. I was still so connected to the belief that I needed the approval of my husband that I chose to let go of my healing. He approved of me being sober, but to change was to risk his loving the new sober me. I thought that I so desperately needed to be loved by him.

David took me to the hospital for a complete medical evaluation, and a probable concussion was decided. I was too embarrassed to admit to having been raped. My brain felt like it had a terrible bruise, and it hurt. After the ER visit, David took me home. I went straight to the bedroom. I felt so dirty that I could not even sit on the bed, so I sat on the floor with my knees drawn to my chest.

David followed me into the bedroom and said, "After all I have done for you, you have done this to me!"

I asked, "What have you done for me?"

He answered, "*I stayed!* And God knows how hard that has been!" then he walked out of the room.

Something about the tone in his voice and the words that were said rang like a loud gong in my heart and in my ears. I became dizzy and disoriented. When I refocused, I began to ask myself, "How did I get to this place? Where was the mountain top peace? Where were the changes that had occurred from having met Christ? Where was my God? Raped a second time, and how could I have ever let that happen again?" There I was on the floor of my own home, dirty, disgraced, raped, judged as vile by the man I once loved dearly enough to marry, almost dying, and all by my own hand.

My soul cried out "I want to live. I will give up whatever it takes to reclaim my dignity, my self-respect, and my life. Even if it means I have to divorce or lose custody of my children. I will live life on life's terms. I will be sober." I did not say this out loud. I just kept it in my heart and followed through with action. I did take drinks after that day, but I never again became drunk.

As I convalesced at home recovering from the mild concussion, I had a lot of time for soul-searching concerning what had happened. I had plenty of time to reflect on my behaviors, my attitudes, my choices, and what was important to me. I had time to dialogue with God and to make some sense of why I felt abandonment by Him. In one of my prayer times seeking God's presence, I had an answer to my questions about why God allow me to be raped as a teenager and again as an adult. I believe God said to me the rapes were the result of broken people making hurtful choices. God has given to mankind the gift of free will so that we are not be forced to accept His love. The agony of free will is that we can use it to hurt others. When we use our free will in this way, God feels agony for His broken children. He suffers along with his children who suffer. That by no means excuses the rapist's actions. They are wrong and the abuser should be held legally responsible. It just helped me to see I was part of a broken world and I have the same power to hurt others. I also have the same responsibility to change my ways as others who, by their actions, words, or even neglect, hurt me. It was only after I could accept that the rapists were themselves in some way broken that I was able to forgive them. My forgiveness of others does not in any way condone what they did.

Three months after the automobile accident, David's employer transferred him to their office in Central Texas. After we were settled in our new home, I began to look for ways that would help me to continue with my recovery program. I decided to return to college, but I was not sure what degree I wanted to pursue. I was able to narrow my focus to that of a ministry through serving as a psychotherapist or possibly the ordained ministry. I met a woman in our church who was working on her master's degree in social work. I had never known about that degree. I thought that social work was a very narrow field. She convinced me that there were many jobs available in the field. I decided an undergraduate degree in social work was where I would begin. I filled out the application and had a copy of my records sent from high school. To my surprise, I was accepted for the following semester. My children were in junior high, and I believed that we could all adjust to my new schedule.

There were a few tasks I needed to accomplish before I started school. First, I wanted to visit Kate's grave. Secondly, I wanted to visit my half-brother, Mark, whom I did not meet at the time I visited with the other siblings. And lastly, I wanted to enter rehab one last time. For my life to be truly set free, I would need to delve into the roots of my alcoholism. I was aware my heart was now open to be rawly honest with myself and to take responsibility for lasting changes.

I went to the cemetery where my Kate was buried. I sat by the grave for hours. I really hoped I would hear some profound message that would fill the hole that had been left there, and this filling would change the course of my life. I wanted to hear all the things I had missed my entire life. I waited. There was only silence. I could hear the wind blowing and smell the freshly cut grass. After a long while, I began to dialogue with her as though she were there. I began to tell her about my life and about me. I talked about the shame that she must have carried because I was illegitimate. I told her how I had carried shame too. I talked for hours. Sobbing, I told her how much I missed not knowing her.

It suddenly occurred to me I was angry that she was not there to answer my questions, and I felt abandoned by her again. The word "*again*" was magnificent. I needed her, and she was not there. I had needed her a long time ago, and she had not been there.

I remembered!

I found that, as the tears flowed, I was able to forgive her for not knowing what I needed. Leaving her grave, I felt purged of resentment and anger toward her. At the grave, I also left the shame I had carried that was not mine to carry. I was able to accept there would always be unfinished business and questions that were never to be answered. I would never know about my birth father. I would never know about their relationship. I walked away from Kate's grave with a profound love for her and connection to the pain she must have gone through for me.

I went to the visit Mark in the prison where he was serving time for actions committed while abusing drugs and alcohol. When I came face-to-face with him, I was struck by our physical resemblance. He stated he too, had had academic difficulties and health problems. He was not able to get either the academic or the medical help that I had been given. He was on one side of the prison screen, and I was on the other. As I sat and talked with Mark, I was aware how much the combination of my biological roots and my environment had influenced my development. I also understood how this unique combination had come together to form my health, my value system, and my faith and had put me into a community that also influenced my formation. It was easy for me to choose social work as my degree plan.

My alcohol consumption had almost ceased. I knew I needed one more detoxification center to fortify me. I chose help from a different style of therapy and a different medical treatment program. My brother found information about Dr. Meg Patterson, from England, who developed a revolutionary medical detoxification treatment program named NET (Neuro Electric Therapy). (Patterson, 1986). I was unable to go to England for the treatment. However, one of the doctor's nurses came to America to give me the treatment in a secure environment. She used mild stimuli to the brain to change the brain chemistry. Minute electrical currents, self-adjusted to a comfortable level of sensation, are passed across the head via self-adhesive electrodes attached on the mastoid process of the ear (located just behind the ear). Continuous stimulation was administered throughout the acute withdrawal phase. The detoxification program was based primarily on highly specific selections or combinations for the different kinds of abused substances. Other frequencies were integrated into the overall program, specific to alleviating my withdrawal insomnia, cravings, depression, anxiety, fear, and agitation. The treatment lasted ten days.

As each emotion surfaced, the therapist talked with me and helped me to process. I was giving validity to my reality. I did not have to stuff any of these emotions like I had from the previous two centers after discharge from treatment. The treatment was rapid, thorough, and safe. A sense of physical well-being, emotional stability, and mental clarity were among the most fundamental and potent of the changes. With such a transition came a profound consequence: a belief that my future could change. With change, everything became possible. And with it, I had hope.

By the tenth day, the nurse asked me if I wanted a drink. I was honest and said yes. She went to the medicine cabinet and brought to me my favorite Scotch. I was told to drink it. I was rather apprehensive, as I really loved the taste of Scotch. I drank it and waited. It tasted really good!

Very shortly, after the Scotch had filled my stomach, I began to throw up the Scotch and continued to do so for a few minutes. The vomit came from the pit of my stomach. I felt like I was throwing up emotions and garbage from a lifetime. Tears flowed down my face, and I kept repeating, "Thank you. Thank you." An overwhelming sense of gratitude washed over me as the tears continued to flow.

From that day to the present, the smell of liquor or beer makes my stomach queasy. Drinking again will always be a choice. For the first time in a very long time, I felt sane. I felt I was able to choose to be sober. I felt clear-minded. I was aware that drinking again would take the sanity away. I would not choose to forfeit that ever again. I discovered the root to my addiction was not only anger, as I had thought, but it was also shame, anxiety, grief, broken emotions, unreal expectations about life, and taking care of others. The major discovery was the realization that I had given up my own identity to be whatever else others wanted of me in order that I might be accepted by them. I had no identity of my own that I could define. I had lost the ability to say what I believed. I had a vision of myself as physically or mentally retarded. I had seen myself as incapable of succeeding. What I believed about the world around me affected how and what I believed about myself. These beliefs influenced not only how I had related to the self, but also how I related to others. I began to look again at the childhood issues and resentments. On another level, somewhat deeper than previous explorations, I became aware of my need to be loved and accepted for who I was when I was as a child. I was able to look into the lives of my parents as individuals and to see their pain. As I identified patterns of behavior and beliefs, it became obvious that I had expected my relationships to heal my past needs stemming from my mother and father relationships. My husband was not and could never be "my father or mother." I had given to him the responsibility of healing me. I made a conscious decision to let go of those resentments and to take responsibility for my own healing.

On Christmas Eve, I left the center with new hope and a healthy sense of well being never again to return to taking a drink of alcohol. I would not forfeit my sanity for a drink ever again. It has now lasted for over twenty-two years.

God had heard my cry in the wilderness. He had brought me safely through the trial by fire. He had provided a way for me to connect with my biological roots. He opened doors that were closed. He saved my life. He gave me hope. He healed me of alcoholism. He had opened the doors so I could reestablish my relationship with my parents, my husband, and my children. He blessed me with a spiritual foundation of rich fertile soil from which all else could grow.

9

A NEW KIND OF EDUCATION

I began my university studies two weeks after discharge from the rehabilitation treatment facility. Challenged by dyslexia, fear of failure, competitive classmates, and the requirement to learn a foreign language, I set my mind and my emotions to the task. All of the tasks required humility, persistence, courage, and the willingness to experience stress. Graduate school was part of my overall plan, and therefore it was necessary for me to keep a 3.0 or better grade point average in my undergraduate studies. Learning time management in family life was difficult at first. Every step of the way, God's Holy Spirit was there to guide and to heal me.

Commuting to the university was an eighty-mile round trip. I was eager to begin, so I enrolled in five classes. Studying for those classes took about twenty hours a week. Getting back in the routine of reading and writing was difficult at first. Our children were in Jr. high and still needed help with after-school activities and homework. There was the usual house cleaning, laundry, and meals to prepare. David and I had an hour or so after the children went to bed and midnight to talk about our day or any problem that needed solving. My study time was wedged into my daily schedule between midnight and 3:00 am. All of the sudden, I was taking care of myself. I was able to tolerate stress without falling apart. The rest of my family gradually adjusted to their new roles of taking care of themselves. At first they were suspicious of my intent and behaviors. If I did not get back from school at the exact time they thought I should, they were worried I was running away again. I needed to earn their trust again. Recovery included the healing of the entire family. My goal was for the healing of the whole family, if at all possible.

My therapist had warned me about possible reactions from family members. The family had learned behavioral and emotional responses to me while I was drinking. These responses had become habits. Change was uncomfortable for everyone. While my family was adjusting to my sobriety, they also were adjusting to the emotional changes in me. In order for me to remain sober, dramatic changes were necessary. I was claiming my right to be me. I was learning how to put my truth into words. I withdrew from caretaking when they were capable of completing their own tasks. I allowed them to be angry with me and to verbalize it. I was willing to talk through situations without falling apart. By the sheer nature of remaining sober, I found I was able to cope with increased stress. I had more energy both for living and for coping. It was becoming evident to me that the roots of healing for sobriety had been formed in all of my attempts to gain sobriety. God had not abandoned me. Every struggle, including the biological family search, had added to my ability to handle stress and to remain sober.

The very behaviors, emotional responses, and attitudes that drove me into alcoholism were to be the strengths that held me firmly in sobriety. Instead of using those for destructive behaviors, I chose healthy ones. I had been loyal to the bottle. I became loyal to sobriety. I had been obsessive and compulsive about drinking. I would now become focused on school and family. I was persistent in behaviors that led to drinking. I used that energy in moving steadfastly toward new choices that ended in healthy behaviors.

Finishing two degrees and the hope of being employed became disputed issues. David believed that my employment would be a reflection on his ability to provide for us as a family. He did not want any part of housework or helping the children with their homework, as he really did not think that my getting a bachelor's degree was necessary. I felt it necessary for my healing journey, necessary for my self-esteem, and necessary for my very life. He made several attempts to convince me that finishing school was in the way of family life. When none of those attempts had any effect, he suggested that we move to another town in the middle of my junior year. This would mean I would have to take longer to finish my degree requirements. I saw it as a sabotage to thwart my successful completion of college. To everyone's surprise, I refused to move. My changes became threats to our marriage. I was becoming assertive and self-motivated. I was changing from being motivated by what others wanted me to be. There was a fine line in securing my path and in accommodating those in my family. The fine line also included the difference between selfishness and self-preservation. I was not sure at that point I was able to complete all my studies and motherly duties effectively, but I was doing my best to learn new skills.

Staying up very late hours to study was necessary. It was the only time I had when everything was quiet and no one needed me to do something. A strange thing happened. When we previously relocated to West Texas, David began to drink alcohol socially. He had not become addicted to it as I had. His favorite was bourbon and mine was scotch. After I started school, David switched his choice of liquor to scotch. I think this response was probably subconscious, but nonetheless, the statement that it made, was the same. Just before his going to bed, he would pour himself a tall glass of scotch and water. He would come by the table where I was studying, kiss me goodnight and leave the glass of scotch at the end of the table. The first night he did that, I thought it was a mistake. However, when it became routine, I would hear the words of my therapist ring out, "Expect sabotage."

Each morning I would mention to him that he had left his drink on the table and he could pour it out. In spite of David's reasons for leaving the glass there, I grew to see that glass as my victory over my desire to drink. He honestly wanted me to be sober and to live a life of sobriety. But he was not prepared for the changes I was making in myself. He wanted that old Jeanne back—the one who had, more often than not, forfeited her needs or wants for whatever some one else wanted, the woman who gave of herself until there was nothing left to give. The giving woman was the person he loved. He treasured my ability to mold my love and life to meet his needs and the world around us. I had given so much that an empty vessel had developed. There is a vital difference between the illness of co-dependency and that of true Christian compassion. I had been a sick co-dependent.

Somewhere along the way, I lost the person who was created in the image of God's son. Discovering this person again was a struggle and required hard work. My life depended on finding her again. I believe that David did not evaluate our relationship as I did. Leaving his glass of Scotch there may have meant that he wanted me to be close to him again as when we first married. My heart, also, yearned to be close to him again. Neither one of us knew how to say it. We had been in love and we were so happy when we first married. Both of us were grieving the loss of our relationship and what it could have been had circumstances been different.

David slipped into a depression of his own. I was growing, changing, becoming self-confidant and verbal. He withdrew inwardly, not seeking any emotional help from anyone. It was no longer healthy for either of us for me to be his caretaker and provide his emotional work for him. I could not be both in counseling for my issues and counselor to him. Anytime one partner changes, it affects the way the other responds. Change requires a response. Change is scary. I ran out of patience with his inability to change. Had I been in a different place, and had I been able to wait until he had had sufficient time to change, maybe the marriage would have survived this crisis. I just could not do the work for both of us. My life was taking on a completely different shape from what it had been in the past.

By this time, I had already worked on my issues in therapy for close to five years. I had neither the energy nor the desire to work on our marriage. We were at a crisis point, and I could not save both of us. We grew farther and farther apart. He had stayed with me during my drinking days and now I was not wishing to stay with him. He said that to me so many times. At the time, I felt like I had to choose between abandoning him or me. I felt so guilty for wanting to abandon him. I tried to fill my days with classes, homework, and helping the children in an attempt to postpone those feelings. I hoped that time would heal our marital stresses.

Healing came in so many ways during my undergraduate time. The first semester back in college, I actually made the Dean's List. I was satisfied that I could achieve the scholarly excellence. I decided I would be a solid "B" student, relax, enjoy the school experience and to have fun with my family. I did not need to make the Dean's list ever again.

The semester following the Dean's List award, I made a thirty on my first test. Oh, I was so embarrassed! Oh well. I showed steady progress through the course, and although I did not make the actual grade, the professor gave me a C because of the effort.

Many times, I would make the top of a grade bracket and the professor would bump the grade to the next letter. They all knew how hard I was trying. I received these grades as gifts, which helped me to attain my desired overall grade point average.

Learning Spanish was a challenge. I can remember times when I would run out of class in tears, not because of something the teacher would say, but because I remembered something about my elementary days—especially the first grade, when pronouncing new words was so humiliating. Then, I had made so many mistakes and would pronounce words incorrectly, and I had felt mortified. The Spanish teacher never did make fun of the pronunciation nor did my fellow students. I was learning I could actually say and make a mistake separate from believing I *was* the mistake.

In all classes, we were required to give oral presentations. Performance anxiety and I were very good friends. Fearfully, I would stand before my classmates, clutching to my report, with sweat rolling down my face. My voice would quiver as I attempted to read aloud. To my surprise, no one made fun of me.

I had been given the gift of motivation and stamina. Persistence followed very closely. I felt the presence of God's Holy Spirit every day in all situations and through each decision. The Spirit was my counselor, guide, comforter, and protector. He even found me parking spaces and paid my tuition. I started with my undergraduate work and attended class through the summers and on through the Master's program. I finished in three years, even with having to miss classes due to a bad case of pneumonia and surgery (another bout of endometriosis produced a small tumor that needed to be removed). I look back on this period of time and I am amazed I was able to finish.

The social work curriculum required several internships as part of the degree. My first was with a downtown street gang near the university. I was not prepared for the agony in their hearts. Food, games, and a safe place to "hang out" for a while were the gifts given in the downtown sanctuary. Most of the teens were living on the street. Many did not know who their parents were; and if they knew, they did not know where they were. Many had run away from home, as home was an abusive place.

These teens were hanging on to life the best way they could. Their gang was their family. It gave them an identity, recognition, a sense of belonging, and what they defined as "love." They would steal for the group, and the money or goods were shared in a pecking order. Once a member of the gang, there was no way for them to leave. Their lives would be threatened if they talked about leaving—death, for sure, if they did leave. Out of fear, members who might have wanted to leave stayed together. As a stranger, I was not to be trusted. Gradually, the fear in the teens' eyes softened. The fear was replaced by caution. I was told by the teens that if they saw me on the streets and were told to do so, they would kill me. There would be no mercy, not even, because I was helping them in the basement of the church where we all met. I would go home at night to my warm bed and enough food on the table to satisfy my stomach. I had a family who loved me. My heart was filled with compassion for those children on the streets fighting for their very existence.

In the second internship, I was placed in an agency whose primary focus was to assist families who had given birth to a baby with a birth defect. The agency provided diagnosis of the defect, counseling, and resources to help take care of the baby should special needs arise. Having a perfect baby to bring home from the hospital is everyone's dream. When this dream falls apart, it can be devastating for the entire family. Many a mother blamed herself for doing something wrong or for being defective herself. Husbands felt similar feelings but rarely verbalized their emotions. They would feel more comfortable expressing anger toward someone else. Feeling responsible for passing the defect along to their child was more than unbearable. A faith crisis almost always arose. The parents believed that God, as the author of all creation, was ultimately responsible for this action. A cycle of rage and then depression seemed to be a consistent cycle before acceptance. Acceptance generally meant the acceptance of the responsibility for, but not necessarily the acceptance of, the birth defect. Needing to find a reason *why* prevented, in many cases, the mother from bonding with her newborn. Marriages were torn apart due to the stress and the blame game. With genetic counseling, psychotherapy, and faith explored, mothers began to put back the shattered pieces of their lives. As the children grew, they had questions of their own. Why am I different? Can I have a normal life? The answers to these questions were never resolved by simply answering the questions. The process to accept one's self is a long journey. I carried a special sensitivity for these children. I felt a sense of oneness with them in their struggles to be *normal.*

The third internship was in a women's hospital. Cancer, adoption, stillborn babies or babies who died soon after birth and reconstructive surgery were among the few issues that were routine. All experienced the loss of life as it had been. All had losses that were unexpected. All grieved. Many had a faith crisis. Families were torn apart by the crisis of loss. Once the patients left the hospital, they were faced with the business of rebuilding meaning to their new lives. I admired the courage of these women.

I remember one such woman. As the result of giving birth to a stillborn, she sank into deep grief. The philosophy of the hospital was that it was emotionally healing for the mother to see, to bond with, and then to let go of the baby. The neonatal nurse with a bundle of what looked like towels in her arm grabbed me one morning and took me to a patient's room. She introduced me to the patient. She put the bundle of towels just at the foot of the patient's feet. The nurse said to the patient that I would be sitting in the room as a presence, so in case the patient needed anything, there would be someone there to assist. As I sat quietly in the corner, I made sure that my breathing was in rhythm with hers. I did not want to be a distraction to her healing process. In time, she brought her knees to her chest, curling into a fetal position. She began sobbing while she rocked back and forth. Eventually she reached for the bundle and continued to rock, sobbing while she brought the bundle to her heart. When she was ready, she was able to stretch out her legs and place the bundle of towels in her lap. She gradually opened the towels and began to see her baby. The mother began to tell her baby the story of her life and what she was going to miss because they were not going to share life together.

By the time that the nurse returned, the mother was completely relaxed and able to share with the nurse how much the baby looked like her. I was awed by the presence of mercy and grace. I was awed by the courage of this mother. I was grateful she had allowed me to be present for the holy gift of healing.

David and I continued to experience stress in out marriage. I sensed that we had moved beyond our ability to save the marriage. Nineteen years previous, I had stood at the altar of my church and promised to remain married to David no matter what challenges our marriage held. My parents counseled me to stay with David. It was their belief that a commitment to marriage was far stronger than any personal need I may have. I was failing at that commitment. Shame raised its head again. I did not want to remain married, and at the same time, I did not want to go against my word. Some of my friends said that God's Word said divorce was not an option and I had to stay married. It was not an easy decision. The time of indecision was wrought with fear, uncertainty, blame, and responsibility. I had to weigh the consequences and know there would be persons who would not agree with my reasons or choices.

Torn between these pulls, I spent much time in soul-searching. I fasted and prayed for answers. I prayed for a miracle that would instantly heal both of us. I wanted to honor my promise to God and my commitment to David, Andrew, and Ruth. I would be responsible for the hurt to them caused by divorce. If I stayed, I would spare them that pain. I ran head-on into the realization that remaining married was a death sentence to me and I wanted to live.

The decision to divorce was a lonely one I had to make all by myself. In prayer, I felt the forgiveness for my mistakes and the grace to rebuild my life. Honoring my God and honoring myself required that I live in my truth. With agony of heart, I told David I wanted a divorce and I filed the legal documents.

After talking with his mother, David insisted I had to move out of the home. I had no income and no job. I was still a fulltime student. Ruth, now a freshman in high school, and I left with the clothes on our backs to begin again. My parents co-signed with me on an apartment lease, and I later was able to get some furniture and our clothes. Ruth and I spent the first night in our new apartment on the floor crying ourselves to sleep. By the grace of God, I found a part-time job that gave us enough money for food for our table.

Andrew and Ruth were caught in the pain of divorce. Both children wanted to be with their dad and with me. They wanted us to "just work things out." These were adult problems and were not easily solved. All of us hurt.

When I moved out of our home, Andrew chose to stay with his father. Because both children were at the legal age that they could decide, the courts allowed their decision. Both David and I shared the loss of a child in our home. Andrew and Ruth lost the benefit of being able to share their every day lives with each other. Divorce is hurtful, and every one for several generations suffers in some way.

Dating again presented another situation that caused our children pain. After the divorce, David and I began to date others. The children could accept their dad dating but not their mom. Arguments and hurt feeling flew. Andrew was so angry that he refused to come for overnight visits with us in my apartment. When I had a date, I had to leave my daughter in the apartment alone. Even though she was a teenager, it was not a good situation. She was apprehensive while I was away and would sit up waiting for me to come home. To reduce the opposition and strain, I ceased dating for a while.

It was university policy for all students to take the same exit exam, which really had nothing to do with the student's degree. All students were tested on the same subjects. I flunked this exam! Now what? I had a 3.4 GPA, and I would not be allowed to graduate because of some exam that had nothing to do with my degree. School policy required that only those who passed the exit exam would be awarded a diploma. For those who did not pass the multiple choice exam, there was a written form. As the room full of students gathered to be tested again, I felt a heavy anxiety. This was my last chance. I did pass this one! On graduation day (1987), I was the last student to walk across the stage. My children and parents were shouting for me as I took that miraculous walk. I wept with pure joy that I had been awarded a college degree. What a milestone for a child with a learning disability.

I cried all the way through taking my Graduate Record Examination (GRE). The tears kept me from seeing the questions, so I just marked the little squares as best as I could. I do not believe that I passed. I had applied both to Presbyterian Theological Seminary for a Master of Divinity and to Our Lady of the Lake University for a Master of Social Work. By God's grace, I was accepted into both graduate programs. Because of my decision to divorce my husband, I felt unworthy to enter the ordained ministry. I chose social work.

A few weeks break and I was back in class for more learning. Graduate school was highly competitive. I was told that graduate classes would be more of the same subjects as in undergraduate, but I was not prepared for the increase in the level of academic difficulty.

I found a part-time job to pay the bills, which allowed me to be able to continue with my master's degree program. Adding to the difficulty of the part-time job and the pressure of school was the fact that I was in limbo between filing for divorce and the final decree. Andrew and Ruth were hurting and I felt responsible for their pain. I slipped into a mild form of depression. I would sleep. Ruth would wake me and tell me to get up. I would get up, go into the living area, and there, I would sit on the couch staring out the window. This pattern repeated itself for days. One day Ruth called one of my fellow classmates and asked them come over to talk to me. The friend helped me to take the feelings and the situation and embrace them from a therapist's point of view. I would need to remember what I was feeling so I would be able to relate to my clients in a special way. By the grace of God, I was brought out of depression and back to the business of school. I did cry often, and so did Ruth.

Keeping in touch with Andrew had its own unique set of circumstances. Our divorce was finalized in 1987. David and I remained emotionally at war with one another. Since Andrew was living with David, I would call the house to talk to him. If David answered, he would vent his frustrations out on me. I was not emotionally in a place where I wanted to subject myself to such stress. I had to choose carefully the times when I would call his house. Andrew later said that he felt neglected for my not calling enough. He turned to the mothers of his friends for advice. Even though I understood, my heart still broke.

I was awarded a Master of Social Work in 1988, a testimony to another miracle. I studied for and sat for the first required Social Work licensing exam. The first and the second time that I took the exam, I flunked it. I made a sixty-nine then a sixty-two. A passing grade was a seventy. I was freaking out. The thought of having come this far and not be able to get a license was exceptionally stressful! My employer had said I would no longer be employed if I did not pass. I was under great pressure. I kept saying the mantra, "I am capable of passing this exam, and therefore, I will." Fearfully, I repeated the exam. I did pass! I passed with a high grade and became a Licensed Master of Social Work (LMSW). A second license is required before I could be a psychotherapist in private practice. This second level required three more years of supervised experience and the successful passing of the exam.

I consider myself a shy but friendly person. I have a difficult time meeting new people or interviewing. I have to force myself to be in a group setting. I have a mild case of social and performance anxiety which causes me to avoid public speaking engagements whenever possible. My face will flush, and I get queasy in my stomach when called upon to talk about something in front of people, probably part of the residue left from being humiliated in elementary school. I am able to talk one-on-one very well. However, on one specific rare occasion, I took a chance. I went to a National Association of Social Workers annual conference, not knowing anyone. The people at my lunch table were friendly, and I quickly forgot my nervousness. The following business day, I received a call from the Personnel Director in a psychiatric hospital in East Texas. The offer for that position was based on the request of a person that I had met at the NASW luncheon. I felt stronger emotionally and thought I would be able to walk through any stress that a new town or a new job presented. I had walked through a divorce, earned two degrees, worked successfully in a variety of jobs helping others to sort through family issues and to face health situations, job related questions, adoption, chronic or terminal illnesses, disability, faith crises, rape or other violent actions, grief and losses. The timing was right for me to leave Central Texas; so, I accepted the position. Off I went in 1992.

Moving gave me an opportunity to live closer to my parents' home. After the discharge from the second rehab center, my relationship with my parents had begun to develop in a way that was meaningful for all of us. I felt Mother and I had begun to talk more openly. I was able to accept both parents for who they were and not what I had wanted or needed them to be. There was a sense of freedom when I allowed my parents to be who they were, knowing they were the same people they had always been. I had spent so many years yearning to feel connected with them, and now it was a reality.

10

EVERYTHING IS CONNECTED

I enjoyed living in my new town. The weather had all four seasons. The people were friendly, and I settled in quickly. The joy of working was incredible. I found that I was able to handle a variety of situations under unpredictable stress. There was only one situation that influenced my choice to leave the psychiatric hospital after a year. One day on the ward, five men circled me, all clamoring for my attention. Each one believed that his need for attention was the most important of all. I was unable to meet all their needs at the same time. As they began to become agitated, the circle around me tightened. Their agitation escalated to a yelling match. I was frightened. I remembered my dad screaming at me. I remembered not knowing what would happen then. I did not know what would happen there at the hospital that day. Eventually the men did calm down and everything was all right. I was so unnerved that I spent the evening on my couch shaking from the trauma. I thanked God for showing me again how scared I would get when dad would yell. I had purposely forgotten that part of my life in order to survive. The sheer reliving of the memory triggered by a work experience was healing. I was able to validate the feelings of the scared little child who lived within me. I decided it was best for the patients and for me that I seek employment elsewhere. I chose a position at a physical rehabilitation hospital.

After the required three years of a supervised internship post graduation, I was eligible to sit for the next exam. The exam was routinely given in several regions at designated university sites. Due to an overflow of applicants for the test date I had requested, the upper level exam was scheduled at an alternative site. I was surprised to discover that the alternative site was the high school I had attended! What a coincidence!

Going to Hockaday that day to take the exam brought back so many memories of all the academic struggles that I had overcome. With a deep sense of pride, I took and passed the exam. When the exam was over, I sat on the curb waiting for my ride with tears of joy streaming down my face. I felt an awesome sense of gratitude for having been a student at Hockaday. The Hockaday teachers had believed I was able to learn with higher standards and higher levels of intuition. They had pushed me to reach my limit with support, tutoring in other subjects when needed, a reading teacher, and scholastic incentives. I was given the opportunity to learn, to develop, and to rebuild a healthier self-esteem. They gave me an academic foundation on which to build for the rest of my life. My parents had given to me the gift of being able to attend classes there. While they were not able to reach me to build academic excellence or a healthy self-esteem relating to scholastic performance, they made the necessary sacrifices that enabled me to attend Hockaday. Because of the scholastic foundation I had been given there, I was able to earn a master's level degree and to qualify for a professional license.

In my new town, I found a church home. I began to attend a Bible study for singles, and because of the intensity of the topic we were studying, we made very deep friendships quickly. I had decided never to marry again out of fear of making another mistake. The intensity of pain that had occurred as the result of my decision to divorce was something I never wanted to put others through or experience for myself. The study group had been together about a year when, to my surprise, I found I was developing a "more than friendship-type relationship" with one of the members. Fear reared its ugly head. I began to question my ability to choose and my ability to make a decision. I feared being wrong again. I had lost my ability to trust my intuition when it came to love. Memories of the trauma of the divorce came echoing back. I feared loss of control. I had been single now for seven years, and I was not sure I wanted to give up that independence. My time was my own. My finances were my own. I was concerned I would return to my old habit of forfeiting my right to make my own decisions. I was afraid I would again return to standing in my husband's shadow. I feared the loss of healthy boundaries. I questioned my emotional healing and whether or not I would feel emotionally safe in a new relationship. I feared the rage that went with my previous break-up.

As Dolph and I began to date, I resisted allowing my heart to fall in love with him. I feared if I began to trust him, in a few years or so it would end in disillusionment. He understood my history of alcohol abuse. Even though he drank beer, I did not think that it would bother me.

One night when we had been out on a date, he had a few beers. He usually kissed me good night on the cheek. This night when he brought me home, he kissed me on the lips. I tasted the beer from his mouth; I smelled it, and I remembered! I remembered the entire nightmare. Tears rolled down my face as I sank to the floor with the burden of heavy sadness. I would have to give him up if he wanted to keep drinking.

With intense emotions, I said to him, "I did not think that your drinking would bother me. However, it does. I cannot continue to date you if you continue to drink."

Dolph said, "I will give it up. You mean more to me than the beer."

I said, "This means never again. Not even when you are out with the men. You would come home, and I would still smell it."

He said that he would never again drink beer or anything that had liquor in it. I was so moved by his response and his commitment to me that I fell in love with him without any more reservations.

Dolph and I were both committed to honesty and openness when talking about our feelings. We dated long enough to have arguments, misunderstandings, or hurt feelings and find resolve. We experienced the death of both his brother and my longtime school friend, Beth, and we grieved together. When we were sure that we were comfortable in our communication styles, he asked me to marry him. After pre-marital counseling with our church minister, we set a wedding date.

In November of 1995, Dolph and I stood at the altar of our Episcopal church and pledged before friends, family, and God to love and honor one another forever. Dolph has blessed me beyond my wildest dreams. With him, I feel emotionally safe, an experience I have rarely had. He is sweet and tender. He honors me. He is honest and provides wise counsel when asked. We can disagree and still honor the other's position. He supports and encourages me. We share like goals, such as our love of nature. It is a special blessing for me to have a partner who wants to share the journey in faith with me. I can freely give back to him because I love him. Our relationship gives me a sanctuary in which to grow and to develop. I am grateful that he is the companion of my soul.

Marriage the second time around had some different qualities for both of us. We were more mature. We had developed communication skills that assisted us in expressing our wants and needs. We had a better understanding of who we were as individuals and were not dependent upon the other to make that definition. We chose to allow each other to grow in the direction that life was calling us. Both of us were willing to compromise and to make sacrifices when needed. We did not have specific expectations of a husband or wife role. Finally, my search for my femininity could be defined. I, as a whole person, could embody both masculine and feminine qualities. It was important for Dolph and I to develop the ability to be comfortable in sharing responsibilities. (see Appendix B). We are able to blend, to be individuals, or to seek the same path.

One of the groups that we joined was a spirituality group. A group of people from many different faiths met once a week to explore the dimensions and expressions of spirituality. We learned about spiritual practices in many other traditions. We went on multiple retreats to further our experiential learning. The more I learned about other traditions, the more I could see God the creator in all things. We learned to appreciate and expand our own spiritual practice. Reverend Gene Baker, a wise Episcopal minister and spiritual director, who was a licensed therapist with a Jungian orientation, led the group. He led retreats and experiential learning pilgrimages. We left hardly any topics unexplored. He provided spiritual direction or psychotherapy when asked to do so.

Another group that we became members of was called The International Order of St. Luke the Physician. The OSL is a body of Christians who believe that the healing of the body, mind, and spirit is a vital part of the total ministry of Jesus Christ. In our meetings together, we read passages in the New Testament exploring specific accounts of Jesus' healing ministry and answered questions related to the passage. When we had finished the readings, we offered prayers for healing. We prayed in teams of two or three. Prayers were to be guided by God's Holy Spirit. It was the Holy Spirit that brought wisdom, insight, and healing. We were the vessels for healing. We were witness to the gracious blessings of God to His people.

Through these groups, my faith grew deeply in a direction that I had never grown before. I began to delve into the mystery of God in an ever-broadening and deeper way, which led to my ability to hear God in ways that were surprising.

One afternoon I was sitting in the doctor's waiting room when the strangest thing happened to me. I use my dreams as a way of understanding my heart and intentions. I had a dream, but it was in the daytime, and I was in a public place. All of the sudden, I lost the sense that I was in the doctor's waiting room. I was outside in the Northern part of the world. Snow was everywhere, but it was not snowing. It was cold, but I was not cold. There was a hill covered with snow, and to the side a forest of trees with birch-looking tree trunks and dark green spruce-like leaves were also covered with snow. Out of the woods appeared the most magnificent pure white wolf I had ever seen. Its white fur glistened in the sunshine. Its eyes penetrated my heart as it looked directly into mine. I felt loved, and I felt that the wolf was kind, gentle and resembled in its nature the Beloved Jesus. Without using its mouth, it began to convey a message to me. It asked me if I would go with it to a place that I had never been before. Because I felt I was in the presence of The Holy One, I said yes. When I did, I began to see sparks of light flash and dart from one tree to the next. Then into my vision came rocks, bugs, planets, and people. The light reflected its spark off all these things as well. The message was that we are all connected by the essence of God and God's loving hand. Everything then became emerald green and pure blue at the same time. The beauty of each color tone was unlike anything that I have ever seen on this earth. It may be here. I just have not seen it. Then I realized that I was back in the doctor's office, sitting in the waiting room.

Where did I go? Was it just in my mind? Was it just a daydream? I have no idea. No one in the waiting room told me that I looked weird or asked me if I was all right. No time had passed. The dream had happened outside time. I called Reverend Baker, my wise friend, to ask for counsel about this experience that I will call a daydream. We discussed how things are connected. For example, letters make words, which make sentences, which make stories. The notes to music when put together make songs or symphonies. DNA put together makes creation. Trees are made of the same elements as rocks. The earth is made of the same particles that are in outer space. Hildegard of Bingen said, "We are all sparks of the Divine." The essence of God's love transforms each of us into a new creation. This newness within transforms those around us. And in transformation, we move back toward God.

Joy is connected to sorrow. Pain is connected to relief. Love is connected to hate. Every action is connected to a reaction. Everything in my life has been and will continue to be connected to every other event. Every emotion is connected to all other emotions. All persons that have moved through my life are connected to me and I to them. I am who I am because of their influence. Everything that goes out from me returns in some way. The unresolved issues in my life go out, possibly hurting others, and return in a painful way, hurting me all over again. Blessings sent out return to bless us. What choices will I make now that I have these new understandings?

Reverend Baker and I discussed the white wolf as a sacred symbol in Native American spirituality. Since I am of Native American decent, what significance could this heritage bring into my life? The white wolf represents courage, strength, intuition, perseverance, the pathfinder, the shadow, and loyalty. Reverend Baker helped me to understand this experience as a call to listen to my own true inner voice—the voice that is not ruled by what society thinks or what I think other people think. I, like the wolf, am not aggressive but can be if called upon to be. Another possible understanding is about knowing my inner power in such a sure way that I do not need to demonstrate it. The wolf comes out at night to howl at the moon. The moon represents my deeper, hidden side, and continued exploration and verbalizing will bring forth the unknown so that I may understand it. We discussed these thoughts as they related to my life's direction. I had much to ponder as I began to awaken to new possibilities.

All of life is sacred. There is no part of life that is not part of the sacred all. While some of the experiences are painful and perhaps degrading, they have the same overall value to the whole, as the wonderful and mysterious events and insights. For you who have had a most devastating experience, you may be shouting in your soul, "No! That is not true. How can this that has happened to me be part of the whole? And there is no way that it is part of what was sacred!"

Your very life is sacred. In my vision of the wolf, it was a surprise to me that all of life was part of the wolf itself. All life came from the essence of that magnificent animal. If the wolf is a sacred representation of the Creator God, then it follows that we are all part of creation as well. The hurtful can become the beginning of the healing process. Thus the hurtful is, with time and healing, a part not the only focus.

Reverend Baker and I concluded that the gifts of special experiences have meaning, which continue to grow as our lives unfold. Many years later, I would move into another dark valley of the night. Each of the days of incredible pain would be connected to each other and to the deeper meaning of my life. I will always marvel at the wonder of the beauty of the wolf and my yearning to remain connected with it. Like the first encounter with the Light of Christ, I felt I was home and wanted to remain there.

As I continued my search for a deeper meaning to my life, Reverend Baker suggested that I attend the Anglican School of Theology, in Dallas, to become trained as a spiritual director and in pastoral care. This knowledge would broaden my personal life and my professional skills. The pursuit of knowledge and the application of this new truth would, by its very nature, continue to transform me as I journeyed into all areas of my life, allowing God's light to shine on them. Spiritual direction is not about a specific religion or doctrine, but about a relationship with God. (see Appendix C).

Dolph and I had been married about a year when Mother called me for help. Dad, by his continued use of alcohol, was rapidly deteriorating. He had caught the kitchen on fire attempting to cook dinner. He had caught the car on fire as he was attempting to recharge the battery. Mother and Dad lived on a private lake. Dad had waded out into the muddy part of the lake and sunk to his knees in the mud. He was unable to pull himself free. Mother placed cookie sheets end to end attempting to make a pathway for her to walk on to try to get close enough to Dad to rescue him. What kept Mother from sinking into the mud is a mystery. Both of them were eighty-four years old.

Mother was also providing care for Martha, whose multiple sclerosis was continuing to progress. Martha was now confined to a wheelchair and needed help with some activities of daily living. Martha's sleep schedule was not like everyone else's. She slept between 3 a.m. and noon. Mother was providing care for my sister and was worried about Dad's safety during the day. Mother would be unable to sleep because Martha would call her and need her to come over to her home in the middle of the night. Mother was exhausted beyond her ability to physically or emotionally cope any longer. She called me to come rescue her.

I remember fearing my feelings as I contemplated going to help Mother. I feared I would literally crumble into nothing if I faced the depth of my love and sadness for Mother and Dad. Nevertheless, I risked facing it. I knelt by my bed and prayed that God would hold onto me even if I shattered into little pieces. I invited God to come into the middle of the broken mess of my situation and be present as I accepted that I loved my parents. I felt an intense weight push me down toward the floor and I could do nothing but sit on the floor. While I was still in tears, the weight lifted. I could return to the kneeling position and realized I did not crack into little pieces. I was able to admit in my heart that I loved both of my parents. I had no idea how much.

I did go to be with Mother. With the help of a family physician, Dad was committed to a psychiatric hospital for detoxification. Mother discussed with Martha and me her thought that Dad needed to be placed in a nursing home once discharged from the hospital. They had been married for sixty years and had been through many struggles. However, it was Mother's call. Therefore, I honored it.

Commitment to the psychiatric hospital was to be Dad's third attempt for sobriety that I knew of. At age seventy-eight, he had gone through the Rehabilitation Center in England mainly because he had been so impressed with the way that I had been able, as the result of that treatment, to live a sober life. He had returned from England and was able to maintain sobriety for a few months. However, he returned to his choice to drink. In a weak moment, to please his family, Dad agreed to admit himself to a second rehabilitation center. Mother had found a center in California that treated alcoholism as a duel diagnosis, alcohol abuse and depression. This second time, I escorted him, now eighty-two, to California and went through the admission process with him. Once I returned home, Dad had changed his mind and wanted someone to come back and get him. He became very angry when no one came. After three weeks, he returned home and continued to drink.

Both of us had walked the journey of alcoholism together. I felt a special closeness to him because of that. I understood his struggles and his failed attempts to gain a life of sobriety. I felt close to him also because of all of our fishing trips we had taken and our long talks. He felt especially close to me as the result of meeting me for the first time in the hotel room with the social worker so many years ago.

On his third day in the psychiatric hospital, Dad went to a hearing to decide if he had to remain there. Someone, preferably a family member, was required to testify that he needed to stay in the hospital because, if released, he would be a danger to himself or others. Since Mother emotionally was not able to go, she sent me. There are no words to describe the burden that I felt.

Committing Dad to this new psychiatric hospital, and then later to a nursing home, was a sad and painful decision. I believed that Dad might have a few healthy years left if he were able to stay sober. His drinking cohorts were not as concerned about his health as his family was.

In spite of wishing I did not have to be the family spokesperson, I went to the courtroom. The judge read the reasons why Dad had to stay in the hospital and then asked for the doctor's opinion and for mine. When I said that I agreed with the doctor—that Dad needed to stay in the hospital—he turned to me and said, "*You, too*"?

As I looked into his eyes, I could see the deep agony of betrayal that he felt. With out any more words, I felt like a knife had pierced right through my heart. I could feel the warm blood oozing out of my chest. My soul anguished for him and what he felt that I had done to him. As Dad was being taken back to his room, his head was bent down, and tears were falling down his cheeks. I felt the weight of the agony of loving him and the burden of doing what I felt was the right thing to do at the same time. Oh, dear God, I hurt!

Before Dad was released form the hospital, Mother filed for guardianship. Dad was no longer capable of making wise decisions about his health or his actions. From the hospital, Dad was moved to a nursing home. He wanted to go home. Even though Dad remained sober and began to have a life of quality and meaning, he remained angry with Mother. He would tell me he felt abandoned and his heart was broken. Mother loved him deeply and I can only imagine the burden of care she carried for Dad.

A couple of years later, Mother called again to say that Dad had a stroke. He had decided to stop eating. He had been hiding his medicines in his shoes without taking them. I went to the hospital to see Dad. With fear in his eyes, his first words to me were, "Is this a nut-house place?" He had not forgotten. I, too, remembered. He never understood the reasons why he was placed in the psychiatric hospital. He had developed alcohol dementia before the stroke. He did not believe that his alcoholism was as critical a problem as it had been. After his health stabilized he was returned to the nursing home and I went back to my houes.

A few nights later, Mother called and said that Dad had taken a turn for the worse and to come quickly. There was a sick, empty feeling in the pit of my stomach. As I was hurriedly packing my suitcase to go to his side, I had a strong and vivid sense that Dad was standing next to me. I could feel the warmth of his body, and I thought that I felt the wind move past me as he breathed.

My spirit heard him say, "I now see my life, and understand that what I did and said hurt you. I love you, and I did not mean to hurt you. I am so sorry. Will you forgive me?"

My heart felt that he fully understood and he was truly remorseful. Without hesitation I responded, "I receive your apology. I forgive you." Well, the most miraculous thing followed. It was as if a lightning ribbon (similar to the ribbon effect of the ribbon candy at Christmas) moved into my heart and pulled out all resentment, all hurts, and all residue of negative emotional pain. The memories of details remained, but the negative or painful feelings no longer had control in my heart. What we forgive on earth will be forgiven in heaven. I was set free. Love for my dad remained and a compassion for him exploded. His presence then disappeared. I later discovered that my experience was just after Dad's time of death. What happens after death remains a question. I am not a theological scholar. I just have my witness to an experience that leads me to believe there is healing in and through death.

After Dad's death, Martha began to have what Mother called multiple sclerosis flare-ups. She saw things that were not there and heard things that others could not hear. She might see and hear people from her T.V. that was not turned on. She might hear or see people running around outside her home. She might see bugs crawling everywhere.

One afternoon, late, Martha was outside her home in her electric wheel chair. She thought that she saw little crawling bugs everywhere. They were crawling on the ground and up the pine trees. She got gasoline and matches. She poured the gasoline out on the tree trunks, and as she bent over to light the tree, she fell out of the wheelchair. The yardman passed by and saw what was happening. He ran over to her and stopped the lighting of the tree and possibly her, too. She was confused and disoriented.

Chad had moved back to Mother's home (1999) after the death of Dad (1998). He was in a life transition and wanted to be with Mother so that she could help him reevaluate his life and his future. He was also a witness to all of Martha's strange behaviors. He was so concerned that he called 911 for help. When the ambulance arrived, Martha denied that anything was wrong and refused medical intervention. With the ambulance still on the property, she made her own 911 call claiming Chad had a gun and was about to harm her. The police arrived on the property with sirens blaring and lights flashing. My brother was then treated as a perpetrator and ruffed-up a bit. Mother was a witness to all of this, and she sat in tears as Martha accused Chad of aggressive actions. Martha was convinced Chad was trying to harm her. There was no gun to be found anywhere. All Chad was trying to do was to get her help. When a person is having a psychotic episode, it can be very scary for everyone. Calling for medical help was an appropriate action to have taken.

11

HEALING OF MEMORIES

As the winter of 2000 set in, so did the pain in my hip. It was not the usual kind of cold weather pain. It was more intense and took more of my energy to tolerate. I had a difficult time focusing on work and making decisions. I struggled to get through the day. My nights became restless and my body began to fatigue from lack of sleep.

That fall, Mother had discovered a lump in her breast. I took off work to take her to M. D. Anderson cancer center for an evaluation. The results of the tests verified that Mother had breast cancer and the cancer had already spread into the lymph glands. A mastectomy and the removal of the malignant lymph glands were the very minimum recommended. Chemotherapy and radiation were discussed as precautionary follow-up treatments. Mother, at eighty-six, had dedicated herself as the primary care person for Martha. She had hired a healthcare worker to provide the heavy lifting, but Mother was there twenty-four hours a day to take care of whatever my sister needed. Martha was a night owl. Her sleep pattern remained the opposite to that of Mother's. If my sister needed anything, Mother would get up and go over to Martha's home. Mother told me she had made a pledge to God, that if He would give her a baby to adopt, she would take care of him or her no matter what. Therefore, Mother labored in her self-giving. She was worn out from the physical schedule she was keeping. She was worried about Chad, who still lived in her home, and spent hours thinking of ways that she could help him put his life together in a meaningful way. Her burdens were heavy.

In her spare time, Mother played the piano, was actively involved in her church and social groups, and cared for all of her plants. She lived a life of service to others, and it was difficult for her to receive help. She loved life and did not want to die. She felt a deep sense of being needed by Martha; and she told me that she was afraid that Martha would not be able to take care of herself alone.

Mother wanted to retain the quality of her life, so she therefore refused chemotherapy. She was concerned that having a mastectomy would interfere with her ability to play the piano. Mother reluctantly agreed to have surgery. To combat her fears, she increased her piano practice time. Mother was grieving deeply. She held in her feelings until she could put into words her grief. The diagnosis of cancer was very sad news for us. It is difficult to be told that someone you love has cancer. We were all grieving in our own ways. We talked about her concerns, and we cried. We talked about options and consequences. A deeper relationship with her was beginning to develop for me that I had no idea would have been possible. Mother began to humbly verbalize her feelings to me.

After my adoption search, alcohol recovery, and college, Mother and I had begun to develop a meaningful friendship. I was able to accept that her goals for my life were noble. She wanted me to develop all the talents that were available to me. She wanted me to have culture and style. She wanted me to be educated. She wanted me to attain a happy and successful life. Her behaviors that used to upset me were diminishing in power. I was able to just let them go. I noticed she was being more forthcoming with praise and attention. Her counsel seemed to have wisdom I needed to hear. As our relationship began to deepen, I wanted to explore the possibility there might be any remaining emotional wounds. I decided to go for therapy because I wanted to identify those areas and find healing before Mother became too ill for us to talk about them. The problem I carried in my relationship to her was in my reaction to her based on my misperceptions and on my unmet needs.

Since I was going for therapy, I wanted to seek assistance for a second issue that had plagued me. I would freeze when speaking in front of groups, and I wanted to be able to relax and to share the wealth of experiences I had gained over the course of my life. The decision to go to therapy was a difficult decision to make because I heard the inner voice say to me, as a therapist, I should not have any problems and being in therapy would interfere with my reputation as a qualified professional. However, I went anyway, as my relationship with my mother was most important to me. I had no idea how I was about to be blessed through this therapist and her style of therapy. It is called Eye Movement Desensitization and Resolution (EMDR). (Shapiro, 2001, 2002).

By using EMDR the therapist was able to by-pass my defenses, my confusion and my loss of memory to penetrate the deepest levels of my awareness. Her style encompassed work on multi-levels all at the same time. (see Appendix D). In theory, the body remembers everything; it holds memory about all experiences. Those memories many times resurface as physical symptoms when the memory is triggered.

Memory also surfaced in the form of emotions, which create an emotional and/or physical response. The decisions I had made about myself were based on my cognitive and personality development at the time the situation occurred, a history of the events that had gone before, and my ability to cope. Memory can be distorted, leading to the composite of details from one event that are put together with another, creating a whole new story. Not all memories are true. They are only our perception of the truth. This new memory became the truth that I remember. I formed a belief system about the world around me and myself and based my life on that memory.

The therapist focused on changing the negative core beliefs that I believed were true. A therapy session might begin with an emotional response, a body sensation, or even a situation in the present that had triggered an exceptionally strong response. It might also begin with an identified negative core belief such as, "I am worthless." The multi-level approach worked deep within my understanding and emotions to provide closure. Sometimes several sessions were needed for completion. Many times, a memory or an event in one session would trigger another related event and so on. Memories would continue to surface in the days between therapy sessions.

I thought my past had been resolved, but there were many issues that resurfaced in therapy. With each healing, I found a deeper level to be discovered. My life experience was like a kaleidoscope to be viewed from many different directions. When examined, each direction offered a new healing potential. I found resolution in my body, in my belief system, in my emotions, in my choices and in my spiritual formation. I had not expected to experience such intense therapy. Many memories had been buried deep within, festering with infection that oozed into and onto my life.

In the first session, the therapist said to me, "When a disturbing event occurs, it can get locked in the nervous system with the original picture, sounds, thoughts, and feelings. The material can combine factual material with fantasy and images that stand for the actual event or feelings about it. EMDR seems to unlock the nervous system and allows the brain to process the experience. That may be what is happening in REM or dream sleep—the eye movements may help to process the unconscious material. It is important to remember that it is your own brain that will be doing the healing and that you are the one in control."

Since EMDR reprocesses negative beliefs that are held in memory, the therapist handed me a list of negative statements to look over. To begin, I chose the statement "I am a disappointment." I was seated comfortably on the therapist's couch. She asked me what memory came to mind and I said, "There was a time when I was six years old and I was experimenting. I was making my mother's eye drops smell good. I put perfume in her eye dropper container. When she used the drops, they burned her eyes. She asked what I had done to the bottle. The expression on Mother's face made me feel she was disappointed in me for what I had done." I believed at the time I made the decision I was a disappointment to her. The emotion that surfaced in relationship to that belief was sadness. For healing to be complete, it was necessary for me to change the old belief to a positive acceptance that I was acceptable as I am.

The therapist asked that I hold in memory all of the above, and then she moved her hand from side to side. My eyes followed her hand movements. As my eyes went from side to side, my imagination zoomed at warp speed to being inside Kate's womb. I saw gray shadows. I felt warm, safe, frightened, and sad. When I sensed I was confined and could not move around very well, I began to panic. My heart began to pound, and my hands were shaky. I broke out in a cold sweat. The therapist kept moving her hands for my eyes to follow. She reminded me that what I was experiencing was already over. I saw a black tube. I sensed a twisted contortion of my body along with more restraints, then freedom. However, there was no one there to hold me. I saw no one. I felt all alone. Where was the person who would protect my life? I was afraid that I would cease to exist if I could not find that someone. My body was cold and empty. It shook with fear as I went into a panic attack. I was a newborn, vulnerable to life and no one was there. I also had a strange feeling of separation and not being connected any longer. I was exceptionally sad. The therapist stopped the eye movements at this point. I was worn out emotionally. She asked me what was the strongest part of the experience. I said the feeling of "exceptionally sad."

She asked me to hold the "exceptionally sad" feeling, and she started moving her hands. I saw Kate hand me to another person. I felt grief that was deeper than I had known was possible. I felt her grief as she gave me up, and I felt mine for being separated from her. I began to sob. My body hurt all over as I continued to sob. I bent over and held my stomach. I thought it was going to be torn apart. I rocked back and forth, as I continued to sob. The experience of loss was very powerful. I felt the loss down into the bone marrow of my being. The memory had lodged itself physically and emotionally in my body. Eventually I stopped sobbing.

When the tears ceased, we processed what had just happened. I came to know that I had carried in every aspect of myself the memory of being separated from the most intimate relationship that exists. I spent the next week continuing to grieve being separated from Kate. Tears would flow unexpectedly, and I seemed to have no control when or for how long the tears would fall.

The next session began with the therapist asking me if I felt there was any unfinished area from the last session that I wanted to revisit.

I said that I had felt abandoned.

She asked me to tell her more about that feeling.

I said I had wondered if there had been something wrong with me and that was the reason why I was given away.

She asked me if the statement " I am permanently damaged." describes what I believe?

I said, "Yes."

She asked me what I felt about that, and I said, "I feel shame." She then asked what my body felt like. My body felt flush in the face. My head wanted to hang down to my feet. I was sick to my stomach. Sharp pains ran through my right hip and leg. I was very uncomfortable, which caused me to wiggle with random motions. The therapist asked me to hold in memory the negative thoughts and the body sensations and to follow her hands with my eyes. My face became so hot I thought it was going to catch on fire. Multiple visions, body sensations, and emotions flashed before me: I saw myself in front of a classroom in tears. I felt naked and exposed in front of everyone. I saw myself looking into the mirror and seeing a twisted and grossly misshapen body. I felt an intense desire to be out of my skin. I felt the painful penetration of the rape incident. I started shaking and moaning. Stop! Stop! Stop!

The therapist reminded me that this was not happening now and that it was already over. Continuing with the eye movements, I anguished over the words of my former husband as I reheard him say "I stayed, and God knows how hard that was." Then I drew a blank. The eye movements stopped, and we discussed the predominant feelings and body sensations that I was having now that the eye movements had stopped. I identified it as feeling naked and exposed. The therapist asked me to hold that feeling and to follow her hands. I saw Martha talking me into things that I did not want to do. My body felt foolish, and I became enraged. The rage elevated so intensely that I screamed as I remembered the time when Martha was allowed to keep waking me up at night while on vacation in Colorado.

The therapist reminded me that what I was experiencing was not happening now. It was already over. The intensity began to subside and the eye movements stopped for a brief discussion. The therapist asked me if I was able to go back into any of the incidents and take charge in order to change the outcome. I felt such helplessness that I was unable to do it. The session ended with us talking about shame and many of the areas that shame infiltrated my concept of myself. I was to spend the week journaling about shame.

By the time I returned for the next session, I was angry that I had not been protected from all of the shame I had experienced. Because I now believed so much of my life had been damaged by shame, I identified the lack of protection with the statement, "I am in danger." The opposite I wanted was to believe the statement "I am safe." The feeling was anger. The body sensation blended anger and shame together with rapid breathing, flushed face, clinched teeth, feeling as if I could not breathe, and a choking sensation in the throat. The therapist asked me to follow her hand movements. I saw myself in the middle of a big ocean, drowning, and there was no one to help me. No one cared enough about me to help. No nurturing was offered. I was abandoned in time and space. I could not go any farther into the feelings. The eye movements stopped for us to talk about the insight. I was able to identify the feeling of being neglected. She asked me to hold that emotion and she started moving her hand again. I remembered being in the baby bed, screaming for attention, but no one came. I remembered needing Mother to talk to me about having dyslexia and my self-esteem. I remembered blaming her for waiting so long to get me to the doctor to see about my hip pain. I remember feeling isolated from her love and attention. My body hurt in my hip, in my shoulders and in my neck, and I felt like I had the aches of the flu. Because I began to feel dizzy and disoriented, the therapist chose to use an alternative form of movement. She began tapping my hands from right hand to left hand until the confusion cleared. Sadness replaced confusion, sadness for the empty relationship void of healthy nurturing that I had had with my mother or my father. I had insight into the lack of nurturing by not only my mother and father, but also Kate. I had formulated that my life was not worth nurturing. I had discounted my needs. I had devalued the quality of my life. I had not honored myself.

I walked away from this session with a new feeling of hope that I actually was healing. Although I did not understand it, I just had a faint feeling everything was going to be all right.

I stayed in therapy for a year, addressing many other negative beliefs. One other that I will mention here is my relationship with my former husband. I believed that he also was unable to emotionally nurture me within the marriage. In and after the divorce, I raged against him for his lack of caring about his own children as well. He seemed to pay more attention to his other girlfriends' and other wives' children than his own. I had watched him repeatedly hurt the feelings of his children, and I would come to their defense like a vicious mother tiger protecting her young. However, it did not stop. He did not listen to me while we were married, and he had continued that pattern with his children. I had not dealt with my divorce, my anger with him, and all the unmet needs that I had felt. It was a very painful journey to go into, seeing my part in the failing relationship. With increased understanding, I was able to claim one hundred percent of my half of the failure. Even with claiming responsibility, I was unable to forgive David.

One day, as I was listening to the radio, I heard Willie Nelson singing his wonderful song, "You Were Always On My Mind," I had a personal transformation.

As Willie sang the words, *I'm so sorry I was blind,* my heart heard my former husband's voice, instead of Willie Nelson, say those words. I suddenly believed that David did not understand what was happening to me, and I received an apology from his spirit. As I melted into tears with my own deep heartfelt remorse for my part, I was set free form the burden of resentment. I was able to see that I had given to him the job of taking care of my needs and that was not his responsibility. I realized that I missed him so much. I missed what could have been had things been different. Just like accepting my father's apology after his death, there were no hurt feelings about David that continued to live in me. What freedom! What a lesson! Above all, what a miraculous blessing!

The healings continued as I began to see my mother from a new perspective within my heart. Each time I went into the depth of my hurts, I was challenged to face the wounding in myself, challenged to forgive her and to see how I had also hurt her. The journey inward was painful. The emotional pain intensified the physical pain. I wept often. As I began to see the big picture of her life and my relationship with her, I began to love her for who she was and not push her love away. I came to understand that her intentions were noble, even though I had been wounded. She loved me and did the very best that she could at being my mother. As my heart continued to heal, I began to remember the blessings she gave to me. I began to remember times when she did care for me. I remembered actions of compassion. I remembered times when she was nurturing. I remembered that she loved me. My love and respect for her grew and became the blessing that allowed me to be fully present for her through her illness.

12

DEATH AND RESURRECTION

Before mother's surgery, I went to my orthopedic surgeon to inquire about this new kind of pain in my hip. Usually in the winter, my hip would flare with arthritic pain. However, this year, the pain was more intense than it ever had been. I had begun to drag the leg since it was too painful for me to pick it up to walk. I could not sleep. I became easily irritated. To minimize the pain, I had to increase my fidgeting movements. It was almost impossible to sit in the therapy room for an hour of listening intently to my clients. My pain was nagging for attention. After another x-ray at the doctors office, I was told that it was time for a revision of the hip replacement. The top half of the total hip hardware was deteriorating rapidly. The doctor and I discussed my situation about my mother and I received permission to postpone surgery for as long as the doctor felt was safe. He recommended I use a cane to minimize the weight on the hip. I followed his instructions and bought a cane. The next morning I attended a continuing education workshop leaning on my cane. I found that I could not use the cane, hold my purse, and get the coffee or sweets that were being offered at the workshop. I almost burst into tears. A deep sadness, covered with disappointment, came over me, and I felt so all alone. So many old memories flooded back into my heart. I did not hear much of the workshop presentation. I had gone internal with my thoughts. I was losing my sense of independence as my sense of vulnerability was increasing.

I made many trips to Mother's house to take her back and forth to M. D. Anderson. My heart grieved for all the other patients there and for what they were facing. I cried for Mother and her struggles. I began to notice that Mother was changing more and more to resemble a little child. This insight triggered my motherly instinct. I became very protective of her. As a mother would have compassion for her child, I was aware that I had a similar compassion for Mother. The blessing arose when mother and I began to talk about the true essences of life. We developed a mother/daughter relationship that I previously had only dreamed about but never dared to think was possible.

The day of Mother's surgery, we went together to the hospital. Breast surgery was only a twenty-three-hour stay. When discharged she would return home where she would have home health for wound care. Mother was hurting emotionally as she faced the unknown. I was hurting emotionally for her and all that she was facing. I was in excruciating physical pain. I would break out in sweats as I attempted to move from one place to another. I found myself shaking with the intensity of the pain. It was almost impossible for me to focus on anything other than my pain. It required supernatural energy to focus on Mother and what she was experiencing rather than on me. By God's grace I was able to put my needs aside.

The pain medication did not seem to be successful in relieving Mother's post-surgery pain. She seemed to be mumbling about her leg hurting. When I inquired about it, she was able, through the fog of medication, to tell me about a traumatic event in her life that had injured her leg ending with the death of her horse. Once she could acknowledge the event and the feeling of sadness associated with the event, the pain subsided. She went peacefully to sleep. What a miracle. Even though she was in physical pain, no medication was needed. All that was required was for her to acknowledge the event. As I have said before, physical pain and emotional pain are intertwined, and the body often feels the agony of both without differentiation.

There was no rest from my pain. On a scale from one to ten, the pain level was about nine and a half. It was hard for me to separate the emotional from the physical pain. Mother's surgery revealed the cancer had spread into all the lymph nodes and into the chest cavity. Radiation would buy time but time was running out sooner than we had hoped. Mother said she did not want me to be sad. We had done all we could and it just had not been soon enough. She did not want me to blame myself. I guess she knew that I would. After Mother's stitches were removed, I returned to my home and to work. My brother agreed to take mother back and forth to radiation therapy three times a week. It was very uncomfortable for mother, and she complained of pain. I would drive down to her home on weekends. With each visit I could see that she was becoming weaker. She was losing her hair and her motivation to play her piano.

I moved from using a cane to using crutches as I continued to postpone my surgery date. Finally, my doctor said I could not wait any longer. By now I was totally non-weight bearing using the assistance of crutches. The upper half of the original hip replacement had shattered, and I was in danger of the femur bone protruding into the pelvic cavity. Therefore, I scheduled the surgery. As I have previously mentioned, the initial total hip replacement had been glued in. After this surgery, the doctor told me that in order for him to put in a partial revision (only the top half of the initial total hip replacement, called an acetabular cup), he needed to scrape the old one out from the bone. He said that good bone also was destroyed. Cadaver bone chips from the bone bank were used as bone grafts to fill in the spaces. The pelvic bone was so thin that the doctor said that he could have put his finger through to the internal organs. Had I waited any longer for surgery, the thighbone might have pushed through the hip cavity and into the internal organs, causing life-threatening damage. I rejoiced that there had been no such internal damage, and I recovered as planned. I went to rehab to strengthen the muscles. The rehabilitation physician's assistant admitted me into the rehab program. I did not see the doctor until discharged. I wondered at the time if my rehabilitation plan was specific to the need to be cautious because of the bone grafts. I trusted the process, but I still wondered. Pain levels had decreased. There is nothing to compare to bone pain. Now my pain was about a four on the pain scale of one to ten.

Two weeks after my surgery, Mother had a seizure and almost died. She was taken to the hospital where her doctor told the family that Mother now had a brain tumor and that she had less than six weeks to live. Why no one had mentioned the possibility of a brain tumor to us before is a mystery. Mother might not have gone through either the surgery or the radiation therapy. All she had asked for was some quality of life for the time that she had left. Be that as it may, the doctor placed her in hospice care and sent her home to die. I went to her home to be with her. Both Martha and Chad waited until I was there so that I could tell mother about her medical status. The role I had been given as the family emotional "fixer" continued. It is hard to shake the long-established roles that are assigned to family members. All of us were grieving, and this was beyond difficult for me. How do you say to someone I love, "The cancer has taken over your body and the time has come for you to go home"? I cried as I told her, and she cried as she listened. She did not want to die. She said that she still had much unfinished business. We planned the business she could do while she felt like it. Cousins came from out of town to see her, her friends at the church came to pray with her, she made phone calls, and I wrote letters for her. She took rides in the car to see the flowers or stop for ice cream. She played the piano and listened to music. We hired twenty-four-hour care, since none of us was physically able to lift her. The brain tumor began to cause mother more disorientation and forgetfulness and increased pain. The cancer in her lymph system and moving into the bones in her rib cage was growing rampant and causing great pain. To make matters worse, Mother got the shingles. She was on three kinds of pain medication for the cancer in her bones, for shingles (nerve) and for brain swelling. Her eyes told me she was still in some degree of pain even with all of her medications. Soon she could not swallow her medication; medicated cream was applied to the skin and injections were given as needed.

Martha would roll over in her electric wheelchair from her home for daily visits. She would bring music on tapes and play them for mother. Chad was there to run errands when needed. Being present in the end of a loved one's life has the potential for healing, awe and wonder for the overall plan of life. Mother had many memories that would surface, and we would talk about. She told me about places, events, and people in her life about which I had never known. We giggled and cried together. I was able to tell her how much I loved her and how grateful I was to her and Dad for adopting me. They had given me experiences and opportunities that helped me to develop into the person I had become. I forgot I was recovering from surgery. My physical pain had diminished, and serving mother seemed to change my focus. My suffering was minuscule compared to Mother's. Six weeks went by too quickly.

On the morning of what was to be her last day, a rainbow appeared that stretched across the sky and landed in the middle of her lake. The view could be seen from the window near mother's bed, which was in her living room next to her piano. Rainbows have the awesome symbolism of witnessing to God's faithfulness to His word and to His steadfast promises of His love. It was only as evening time rolled around that we understood the special gift of the rainbow on that day.

As Mother's blood pressure dropped and the signs of immediate death presented, I wanted more time. Please wait! Do not die, yet! There was so much I wanted to say. I prayed that time would stand still. I found that indeed time did seem to slow down, almost to a standstill. I thought I saw an exact image of Mother's fragile body hovering just above her. Her physical body had substance while the other was more transparent, airy, and light. It did not seem to have weight and therefore was floating. I wondered if I were seeing Mother's soul. From her floating image, her eyes were looking intensely at me as though trying to say something. Was I witnessing her soul as it was leaving her body to go to Heaven? I became frozen, as I watched this mystery. At the time, I wondered if I was fabricating the vision in my grief. Possibly my double vision from dyslexia was playing tricks on me or actually serving as a blessing for me at this time. Maybe it was real. If it was real, what did it mean? Was Mother teaching me about what is beyond the grave? As I sat quietly with her holding her hand, she slipped peacefully away (and the transparency also left). In peace and at rest, she let out her last breath.

There was a beauty in her death at her own home. There were no loud instruments going off, no medical staff needing to check in for vital signs, and we had all the time we needed before she had to be taken to the funeral home. Martha, Chad and I sat next to her bed, and we remembered her with laughter and tears. A sense of her presence remained for days. The priest came and gave her a blessing, and then a good friend came with the funeral home personnel to ride to the funeral home. Above all, Mother was in the favorite room of her home with a view of the lake outside and near to her beloved piano.

A few days after the funeral, I returned home. I had been given the task of closing Mother's estate, and therefore, there were tons of boxes with paperwork to go through. The boxes full of documents seemed endless. My sister had a difficult time with me because I had been given the responsibility of executor. I began to hear rumors of things she said about me and her disappointment that Mother had designated me as executor. Martha was distressed she had not been chosen. I think it was mostly her grieving, her disappointment, and her feeling less loved by Mother for choosing the middle child instead of the oldest to close the estate that caused her to voice her opinions. I wanted to change Martha's feelings so we could be friends again, but nothing helped.

Due to the situation with Mother, I had missed the normal six-week-follow-up post surgery visit with my surgeon. By the time I could make the visit, I had begun to notice a strange "click" when I walked or moved. I mentioned this to the surgeon, and after he examined me, he ordered and x-ray. *Yuk!* The new hardware in the hip had cracked loose from the bone grafts, which had cracked loose from my body. Two of the many screws that had been put in to hold the new hardware had broken. I had to have surgery again to replace the damage.

No! This was not fair! Why me? I must be dreaming! The doctor must have looked at someone else's pictures! What happened? Maybe it was the doctor's fault. Were the bone grafts not compatible with my body so that I thus had rejected the transplant? Was the orthopedic surgeon incompetent? A failed replacement! Had rehab been too strenuous? The rehab doctor never examined me so maybe his rehab regime was the culprit. Where was God? My prayer team had prayed for blessings and health to be the outcome from that surgery. We had even prayed for guidance about God's will for which orthopedic surgeon to choose. Had he answered my prayer with a failed surgery? Why would God be responsible for a failed surgery? If He had not answered my prayers, why not? Did He even care? And now, after the death of Mother, I had to go through all of this again! My heart was so heavy. I felt betrayed by the surgeon and by God. I had to start recovery all over again. I was not sure if I could stand another surgery. There would be more trauma to the muscles and the bones. I was confused. I was outraged. I had a hodgepodge of feelings all jumbled up in my heart. I was so disappointed and outraged that I cried and cried and cried.

13

EXAMPLE OF BROKENNESS

I scheduled the surgery date a month away. I felt like I needed to work and have some time to attend to some of the business of my mom's estate. Dolph took me back and forth to Mother's home to get the boxes and boxes of files that I needed to settle her affairs and I began the preliminary cleaning out of her home. We were going to have to sell the home and the property that had belonged to my grandfather to pay the estate taxes. The system is so unfair. My family had already paid taxes on the value of the property and to have to sell now was, in my opinion, a crime.

It was incredibly sad. My grandfather bought the home with acreage when I was about two years old. Originally, a log cabin with a magnificent rock fireplace rising from the floor in the living room was on the property. My grandfather added two bedrooms. We would go there on weekends to get away from the business of the city life. We would have so much fun. We would ride horses and take long walks in the forest. There was a lake on the property where Dad and I would go fishing. He enjoyed taking me out in the rowboat. Dad and I developed a special relationship as we experienced these activities together. Martha and I would find a special spot for the family to have Sunday morning prayers.

In 1969, Mother and Dad moved to the log cabin, relocating from the city. Chad was in high school and completed his education there. Mother built her dream home a few yards away from the original log cabin. Martha moved into the log cabin and began to publish and to print her own newspaper. We all had our own many memories relating to the property. Being back in Mother and Dad's home after her death brought up such sadness in my heart. The empty house felt strange. I did not hear her music. I did, however, sense her presence. The air was heavy. The floor was cold to walk on. The lake had lost its luster. I missed my mother. There were to be no more new memories, no more Christmases, no more learning about her. The more that I missed her, the more my hip hurt. The more my hip hurt, the more my sadness about having to have surgery I grew. I was so disappointed. We did sell the home, and immediately the new owner, without regard to the trees, clear-cut this beautiful property. The one hundred and fifty acres were now barren. I felt like I had betrayed mother.

When my second surgery was over, I chose to go home rather than to a rehabilitation facility. There was more pain after surgery than before. Because of the trauma of the repeated surgery itself, I was suffering. I did not like the new bone grafts. I emotionally was at odds with "something" internally. I could not define it. My doctor told me that he did not know of any reason that my body would reject the grafts. Maybe it was healing and I just was unable to properly identify what my body felt. I did not like the feelings that I had. The scar tissue was tightening and causing burning pain. The sciatic nerve must have been compromised in surgery (a listed side effect), thus the continued burning pain in the back, down the leg and into the foot. I was awake most nights, pacing the floor with my walker, shaking in pain, and crying my heart out. One of the ways that I helped my body to tolerate pain was to move around. I was only able to use toe-touch weight bearing with the walker therefore it was not possible to reduce the pain with movement. Nighttime was so quiet in my apartment. I was emotionally and physically exhausted and feeling panicked about not being able to sleep. I heard all the sounds of the traffic passing by. I heard the neighbors talking outside their homes. I smelled the food from the restaurant across the street. I turned off the lights in the hopes that I would psychologically believe it was time to sleep. But I could not rest.

I moved around in the cold dark night. God had come to me in the night before. Where was He now? I hurt seemingly beyond my ability to tolerate the pain. My husband was sound asleep. We had talked about what he could do and we had accepted there really was nothing that would be helpful. He wanted to protect me from all the agony that I was experiencing, but he could not. I love him for trying everything that he could think of to ease my pain. Even as he accepted his limitations, he still grieved for me. He had loved my mother, too, and was grieving her loss at the same time with me. The doctor tried many different kinds of pain medications including muscle relaxants, and nerve medications, but none provided relief. Even the sheets on the bed caused excruciating pain. The burning pain felt like I was being burned alive.

During the day, I would go through my mother's files reading all the different things that she had stored there. Mother had a box marked "treasures." In it were memories that were special to her. I found pictures of friends, old classmates, and family. There were old letters from her friends and her family and old Mother's Day and birthday cards from loved ones. I found her favorite Bible verses and sermons. As I went through each item and read, I grieved my loss over and over again. I missed her so badly. I wanted to talk to her about what each item had meant to her and learn more about her. My heart hurt during the day and my leg at night. Deep sadness would sweep over me at unpredictable times and catch me unprepared. I cried buckets. Grief is truly the deepest of the human emotions. I did not know if I would ever stop grieving her.

During those weeks, before she died she would say to me, "Oh, I did not know that you loved me." I was so sad because I did not remember that I had told her before she got sick. Going through the boxes of her treasures, I found cards and letters from me that did express to her my love and appreciation for her. A sense of healing washed over me and I knew that the grieving process was healing. Years later, I still miss her. I smell her perfume, I hear her voice, I remember the funny things, and I laugh as well as cry. The thought that came to me was that, since I was grieving her so very deeply, then I must have loved her so very deeply.

Another insight that was born in my deep grieving for Mother was the idea that God feels grief, deeper than what I was experiencing for Mother, for His children when we turn away from Him. I am reminded of the scripture passage when Jesus says "O Jerusalem, Jerusalem . . . How often would I have gathered your children together as a hen gathers her brood under her wings, and you would not." (Matthew 23:37, RSV). Really, the entire story of God, as written in the Old and New Testaments, is a love story of His passionate attempts to reach out to his people.

In my grief, I felt excruciating physical pain. I began to ask my body if the pain that I was feeling was physical or emotional. When I could determine which, I would medicate accordingly. This seemed to be the answer for me. If it was physical, I took the prescribed medication; if emotional, I would sit and grieve until the pain softened. The pain medication made me sleepy, and I did not like to take it during the day for that reason. But, having been up all night in tears from the intensity of pain, I found that sleep is good.

After two months of recovery, I was able to put full weight on my leg. The muscles were not strong enough to tolerate my body weight, which made it necessary to continue to use a cane. I returned to work. The pain medication made me sleepy; therefore, I chose not to take the level of medication needed to stop the pain. As a psychotherapist, I needed to be alert.

A strange phenomenon began to develop. Because I was still in great pain, which could be seen in my eyes, and I was struggling with my cane, my clients felt a special connection to my suffering. Many of the walls that my clients built as protection to hide behind were relinquished. They reported feeling that, because of my suffering, I would understand theirs. I felt honored to be allowed to move with them so deeply into their hearts.

As time passed, my frustration with the pain increased. I began to wonder if I had cause to sue the surgeon or possibly the rehabilitation doctor. The rehab doctor never really examined me for it was his physician's assistant who initiated the rehab program. I sought legal counsel. The lawyer said that he had several claims already filed against the rehabilitation doctor for malpractice and my case should be investigated. I seriously considered his counsel. I remembered some of my clients, who through their own pursuit of legal remediation for wrongful medical intervention became embittered as they also became obsessed with the process. I decided that, even if I were justified in my claims of malpractice by either or both the orthopedic surgeon and the physical medicine doctor, I would not pursue legal action. I was already struggling with such difficultly to heal that becoming consumed with anger would only interfere further with my healing process.

I was losing my belief that God answers prayers. I became angry with God. Who was God, anyway? Why was He so cruel to allow me to hurt with such intensity or for so long? I had been through enough. What kind of God would answer some prayers and not others? I forgot the long history of God's blessings in my life. I forgot that He has always answered my prayers in His time and in His way to secure His outcome. I was surprised how quickly I forgot that He is interested in healing my spiritual life as well as my physical or emotional life. Under the heavy weight of the pain I was enduring physically and mentally, I forgot that God does indeed care about me. I forgot He sees the big picture and I see only a very tiny speck of it.

The longevity and the intensity of pain wore me down, and I became disheartened. I became discouraged about my situation. I lost hope that things would ever get any better. The pain was all consuming and it infiltrated ever fiber of my being. I was irritable toward my husband and did not want to be touched. If he wanted to talk about what was on my mind, I wanted to withdraw. His ability to tolerate the changes in my response to him, because I hurt so badly, was a gift of grace. One of my friends said to me, "what you are experiencing is a stressful situation, and you *should* be glad that it was not an illness. This situation has a solution." While the intent of my friend was to provide comfort, those words just added to the intensity of my pain and sadness. I felt broken and unable to function. I felt I had lost my ability to hold on to a God who answered prayers. I felt absorbed in self-focus because my needs were not quickly resolved. These answers were not happening my way or in my time. Depression led to my inability to push through the pain with the drive that I once had. There were days that I did not want to get out of bed and go to work. I would pull the covers up over my head and say, "I am not doing this today." And yet, I was pulled to reach out to the pain of others. I would get up and go to work. I was unable to hide the physical pain that I was experiencing. My clients saw in my eyes and in the way I walked, that I was in unbearable pain, and thus were assured, that I would understand their pain. They identified my brokenness with their pain. They could relate to me, risk being open and accept the real possibility of being helped.

A special blessing came from one of the ministers in my church who had cerebral palsy. He is both physically and verbally challenged. One Sunday I was standing at the altar rail, for I was not yet able to kneel, with my hands outstretched waiting to receive communion from him. As the broken minister placed the communion bread into my hands, I heard the words—which seemed to be coming from Jesus himself—say, "I am broken *for* you, you are broken *with* me." I felt an overwhelming sense of holiness in my brokenness, oneness with Jesus and with the minister. Healing was not physical at that moment. The healing was deeper than words, for it moved me into a place of acceptance for my brokenness as a blessing. My soul became softer as a result, and the power of that moment was not disabling, but rather, strong, upright, and unlimited. Healing is a promise from God. It came in many unexpected ways.

During this time, I was seeing persons in the role of pastoral assistance. In a particular pastoral care setting, I met a woman named Clara. She had a stroke two years before our meeting. She was a self-made scholar of the Bible and Bible history. She believed the knowledge that she had discovered and the Bible are the absolute truth of God and that there was no room for debate. The stroke had left her paralyzed on her right side. Neither her speech nor her intellect had been affected. She was able to use a walker but mostly remained in a wheelchair. She had been in hospitals, rehab centers and in a nursing home as part of her recovery program. When I spoke with her, she had been home about three months.

Clara believed that God would heal her physical limitations. Yet, her disabilities remained. She would become highly frustrated in her attempts to do physical things that further reminded her that she was still physically challenged. She would get discouraged and become depressed. She was searching the Bible for a miracle as well as seeking alternative medicines and therapies in the hope of finding a cure.

In my conversations with her husband, he was able to share his frustrations about being a caregiver and how difficult it was for him to be truthful with himself and her about her condition. I share my conversation with Clara as tribute to her courage and the struggles she faced spiritually and psychologically:

Jeanne: Hello Clara, how are you today?

Clara: It is so slow. I am just waiting on God to heal me. However, it is not happening soon enough.

Jeanne: I know that I get impatient, also. I also get tired in struggling to work at recovery. Do you ever just get mad or discouraged?

Clara: Yes. I want it right now and all that waiting for 'stuff to get there' has always been a bother to me. I do not like to wait. I have too much to finish with my life to be this way.

Jeanne: What do you mean by saying "this way?"

Clara: I am lame. I have studied the whole Bible, and I read that the lame cannot offer a sacrifice of praise, or be involved in an active ministry. I know God is going to heal me because He knows that it is the intent of my life to praise Him, to worship, and to witness to others.

Jeanne: What do you mean not being able to witness? Is it because you are in a wheel chair?

Clara: I cannot raise my arms in praise. I cannot stand to talk. I cannot play the music by which to sing. I cannot even type on the computer any longer. I am dependent and not giving my whole self in life.

Jeanne: Is healing only the physical?

Clara: That is the healing I need right now. God cannot leave me this way.

Jeanne: Tell me more about this way.

Clara: I cannot take care of myself, I fear another stroke lurking around the corner, or a seizure without notice, and I cannot play my music anymore. I am not *me* any more. Even the simple things are such a frustrating struggle. I have to depend on my husband to take care of the things that used to be my responsibilities. My place as a wife is to take care of him. I feel useless at times. I cannot even go to the bathroom by myself. I get embarrassed so many times.

Jeanne: I share so many of your struggles. I used to be able to carry the watering can to water my loved flowers. Now I need help. There have been many changes in my life, and I have struggled to adjust to them. I do, like I hear you saying, get frustrated and wonder about my value. Can a person be healed in every other part of her life and remain with her particular physical limitation?

Clara: That is not healing. We are promised complete healing, which includes the physical. God is going to heal me because His word says so. I just get impatient because it is not happening. In fact, I feel like I am getting worse.

Jeanne: I have had those times, too. I feel like I am making progress, and then I lose it. Recovery is a struggle for me as it is for you. One of my biggest struggles is that I have seen myself as disfigured. Every now and then, blessings slip in and enable me to keep on keeping on. I have found healing many times is spiritual first and then the physical.

Clara: I still want physical healing. I want to walk. I want to be independent again. I want to provide for my family again. I have lost my identity and do not know what it will be if God leaves me in this condition. My life has been a commitment to serving God, and I do not know how to serve Him any other way. That is an unknown to me. However, God has a way that is not necessarily mine. He has to heal me so that I can return to serving him. I cannot be left this way. I really appreciate that you to talked to me today. I do not have many friends who understand.

Jeanne: Blessings to you and may Jehovah Rapha, the God who heals, be merciful unto us.

With a smile on her face Clara said, "Amen."

Clara did eventually return to her active ministry, although she remained in a wheel chair. She was able to resolve her faith crisis and redefine healing as going beyond the physical. She was able to face her pride and her unwillingness to move into a life of value from the chair. She sang with a passion from a heart that had a quality of angels. She found peace and a new purpose.

This story has a sad ending for her family. Clara developed a brain tumor and passed away a few years later. Clara was at peace and radiant when she passed away.

14

HEALING WITH DREAMS AND OTHER BLESSINGS

In my own struggles in recovery, I have learned much about pain, setbacks, body image, other people's reactions to the disabled, feeling abandoned by God, and prayers answered not in the way I had asked for. I have faced the stark truth that I abandoned God. I have found that there were times in which I wanted to pull the covers up over my head and not face the day. There were times when those closest to me were more of a thorn in my side than comforting. I have struggled with depression, disappointment, disillusionment, doubt, and loss of what was part of me. I have experienced the fear that nothing was going to get any better and the fear that the pain and the limitations I was experiencing would always be with me. I have been angry and resentful. I have wrestled with why God chose to leave me crippled.

If I look at the meaning of all that I was experiencing and thinking, I realized that the healing of my leg also involved the healing of the whole self. Not only my ability to walk, but to walk upright in personal truth—truth that gave me the strength and allowed me to walk in and over treacherous terrain through the storms of life symbolically as well as literally. I was challenged to look into other ways I was crippled in life. Could I trust even in the midst of a dark night of my soul? Could I allow life's experiences to take the necessary shape so that empathy to relate to others in a deeper awareness of love might be born in my heart? Could I break that I might assist others in being set free?

I sought spiritual direction to help me understand what all of this might mean for me and what God might be revealing to me through these questions and symbols. I was torn between the obvious presence of God's blessings in my therapy office and the incredible lingering agony of pain which often seemed to me as if God had abandoned me. In the process of this search, working with a spiritual director, I had two more dreams that are meaningful. The psychoanalyst, Carl Jung, used dreams to help in the healing process with his clients. Many cultures have also used dreams for revelation. Dreams are a natural source for understanding the subconscious. As Shakespeare writes in his *The Tempest* (IV, i), "We are such stuff as dreams are made on, and our little life is rounded with a sleep." Our dreams are made from our own stories and have meaning for us. Dreams that provide healing and offer warnings are documented in the Bible. (see Appendix E).

My dreams are usually composed of a series of images, actions, words, thoughts, and feelings over which I have little or no conscious control. The people, places, and things of my dreams can sometimes be related to remembered life experiences or images that remain in my memory. However, more often they seem to come from sources to which I have little or no conscious access. I believe that we all dream even if we do not remember those dreams. I believe that our dreams are gifts to help us understand our journey in life. Understanding our dreams takes writing them down and working with them to decode its meaning. If I tried to ignore the inner world, as most of us do, the unconscious found its way into my life through pathology: as in physical complaints, compulsions, and emotional stress.

In the first dream that I want to share, I am climbing down into a canyon similar to the Grand Canyon. Down deep I climb, and when I reach the bottom, it is a flat valley. No trees or greenery are present. There is a running stream with light refracting off the water as it rushes over the rocks. There is so much light dancing off the water that it looks as if I am looking into the heavens at night and seeing all the stars. The banks on either side of the stream are wide, brown dirt pathways with rocks along the trail. Then the ground rises dramatically upward setting the boundaries of the canyon walls, exposing all the colors and configurations of the layers of the earth that have formed over the eons of time. I start walking peacefully along the well-worn path by the riverbank. Then suddenly, out of nowhere stands a big brown bear on his hind feet, his arms are outstretched, and his claws are extended. His teeth are exposed as he snarls loudly at me.

I say to him, "What are *you* doing here? Be quiet!" To my surprise, the bear obeys and returns to all four feet on the ground. The bear becomes docile, looks at me lovingly and we then walk along the riverbank together. I feel the brown hair on his back as I move my hand over him. I see the light shining off the hair follicles. We are at peace with one another. We are friends and co-journeymen as we walk along the riverbank together. We walk for a while together and then I awake.

What might this dream mean for me as I struggled to make sense of the pain I was experiencing, the disappointment that surgery had not been successful, my guilt for possibly choosing the wrong doctor, and my crisis of faith? I was highly worried that the pain would never stop. My life was actually consumed with pain. I was paranoid that I might hurt worse. I became very overprotective of where I would go and how closely I would stand next to others. I reacted to any threat of pain like someone with posttraumatic stress disorder. I feared that it would occur even without any real present danger. At just the thought that it could get worse, I would shake with anxiety. On days that the pain increased, I would sink into disappointment that seemed too heavy for me to carry. I considered as a possible interpretation of this dream that the things I fear or find anxiety-provoking could be my friends. I would need to face them squarely and confront them. I felt a sense of empowerment to take action once again. Anxiety could be my friend. Pain could be my friend. I remembered the instruction of my cousin from my childhood—"to embrace the pain." It was harder now to embrace the pain because of the length of time I have been in pain. But, I could do it.

The next dream that I want to share is about a lion. I am in a dungeon-like cave, waiting to be devoured by a lion as punishment for what I believe to be true. I will not deny my belief, and I am going to be the lion's dinner because of my steadfastness. The lion comes into the dungeon and walks over to me. The lion is magnificently beautiful. He is powerful in stature. I know that death is eminent. I surrender to the pain of such a torturous end and accept that my time to die has come. The lion stood for a while, looking at me lovingly and then turns and walks back toward the door. Some men rush into the dungeon and start beating the lion with sticks. The lion does not resist. As the lion begins bleeding, he falls to his knees. He turns his head toward me and seems to say, "I love you." My heart cries out, "It should be me dying. You have given your life for me. Why me?" The only answer is, "I love you."

The multiple meaning of this dream will continue to unfold as my life unfolds. As a beginning, the dream might mean that I fear standing up for my truth out of fear of being destroyed. The dream indicates the possibility that I am not destroyed. There is also the idea that it is a remembrance of the story of Christ and His sacrifice for me. This sacrifice evokes selfless giving. It is also a humble reminder that I am loved. It is a blessing for me to know that there is no limit to which God will go to show me. I could imagine that God must grieve for us as He yearns for us to respond to His loving us. His heart must break when we do not respond to His seeking us for a relationship. In all my forgetfulness, God remains faithful. In all my denying that God is involved, He remains faithful. In all my fear, God is there. In all the times that I abandon Him, he remains true. God shares my pain. He walks with me wherever I go and there is nothing that can separate me from Him. Nothing!

Another thought was that the lion symbolically represented me. The lion's (my alter ego) task was to destroy my decision to stand firm on my truths. The lion decided not to destroy the truth. He decided to allow the truth to live in exchange for his death. The important fact here is I am acceptable as I am.

My fear of pain and the lack of hope that anything would ever be different shifted focus. I could embrace the pains in my life and I would not be destroyed. In fact, I would be liberated by my acceptance.

In late September of 2002, as I leaned over to pick something up off the floor, I felt and heard a crack! Oh no! *Not again!* This could not be! No injury, no over-exertion, and nothing to stress the hip so what was happening? It was too easy for the hip to break loose. Maybe it had never attached successfully. A trip to the orthopedic doctor showed upon x-ray that the second hip revision had indeed broken loose.

I almost had a sense of relief. It seemed strange that I was tremendously disappointed that I would have to go through another surgery. And yet, I was glad that a third time might allow my leg to "feel" right in my body. I had carried around a sense that the second hip was out of sync with my body. The bone graft *felt* wrong, the muscles did not want to walk with a normal rhythm and I hurt most of the time. I still had to walk with a cane due to the pain. I had hoped to be able to resume a lifestyle that would allow me to hike, to carry my own tray at a cafeteria or to put the laundry away. My loss of independence had remained. The list of losses went on and on. So many simple things are taken for granted until they are gone.

Before the surgery for the first revision, I had tried to find Doctor Joe King, the orthopedic surgeon, who had preformed my original hip replacement, but was unable to locate him. I knew the town, but there was no listing in his name. It had been thirty years, and I suspected that he was deceased. My brother asked his cardiologist if he knew of an excellent orthopedic surgeon who specialized in failed hip replacements. His doctor suggested the Fondren Clinic in Houston. I called and asked the receptionist the name of the doctor at the clinic who specialized in failed hip replacements. I was transferred to a nurse. After a brief description of my situation, she made an appointment for me to see the doctor. With great hope, I went to the appointment.

There in the lobby of the Fondren Orthopedic Clinic was a large picture of *Dr. Joe King,* founder of the Fondren Clinic. My mercy, what a blessing, which has been given to me! What a big surprise! It was like God was shouting, "I heard your prayers, and I sent you here." God had been in the middle of my physical pain and in my spiritual and emotional distress. He had not abandoned me. I had an overwhelming sense that this surgery would be successful and that everything was going to be all right. Moreover, it was.

I knew immediately when I awoke from surgery that this new hip was at home in me. I began to walk with a comfortable rhythm, my legs were the same length, and the pain had decreased significantly. The new bone grafts went unnoticed. There was no burning or itching inside. Becky, another one of my friends from high school, surprised me with visits while I was in the hospital. She even surprised me by bringing another friend, Barbie, who was in town for a seminar, for a brief visit. We giggled and talked until we were hoarse. Margaret, also a high school friend, called and wrote letters to encourage me through out recovery. The beauty of my high school friends is that we have remained close for over forty years now. Close friends are more precious than gold or silver. I am grateful to them for their love, devotion, and honesty. We have been there for each other in joy and in sorrow. We had been honest with each another when needed even to the point of risking losing the friendship. The quality of our friendship would not be a friendship without honesty.

Dolph was moved by the devotion our group had maintained over the years. He told Becky she had been a special angel sent by God to be with me every day while I was in the hospital. Her response was, "What a sweet comment! I do not consider myself an angel sent by God, but I do believe He can prompt us to do His will. I do remember having feelings of needing to be there. I did not really try to analyze the feelings; I just knew I needed to be at the hospital. God is so good and faithful. He knows our innermost needs, even before we do. Some forty-three years ago, God 'organized' a group of girls together in high school. We did not know it then, but a lifelong friendship was forged. I praise God and give Him the Glory for those friendships."

I decided not to return to work in 2003 in order to give myself time to heal completely. Since I believed stress had been a major factor in the prolonged and unsatisfactory recovery period of the two previous hip revisions, I wanted to minimize any stress during this period of recovery. I spent extra time in rehabilitation exercising to rebuild the muscles. It took two years to gain strength in the muscles and to be able to throw away my cane. Three surgeries in a year and a half had traumatized the muscles and the sciatic nerve in ways that made me question if they were ever going to return to normal. They ached, cramped, and burned from over-fatigue. Being awakened in the night to walk out a severe leg cramp was common. The muscles were too weak to support me without the continued support of a cane.

After a series of botox shots to the cramping muscles, many trips to the health food store for joint support supplements and continued prayers for complete healing, the muscle spasms ceased, and the pain lessened. Then miraculously, strength returned and the pain almost disappeared. Tears rolled down my face as I embraced the answer to prayer after such a long a wait! Two years after the third revision, I was finally able to throw away my cane. The thrill of being able to carry my own tray again at the local cafeteria was beyond words. I was almost giddy in the cafeteria, and no one knew why. Carrying my own tray was a symbol to me that my independence was back, the chapter of my struggles with hip surgeries was over. How strange our lives are as we go about living each day. We have so much to share with others, and we determine either it is not the right time to do so or that no one else would want to know. Everyone in that cafeteria had their own story to tell, but none of us knew what those stories were.

A home exercise program required me to begin walking on my treadmill and to make a major change to my diet to increase my energy. I was beginning to feel myself again. After a long five years of pain, limited range of motion, loss of my independence, the death of my mother, repeated disappointments and loss of faith, I emerged renewed.

I was reminded of the Bible verse from Isaiah 40:29 and 31 "He gives power to the faint, and to him who has no might he increases their strength. But they that wait upon the LORD shall renew their strength, they shall mount up with wings as eagles, they shall run and not be weary, and they shall walk and not faint" (RSV).

I am also reminded of a story about the eagle's journey as it renews itself. When the eagle finds that it has grown weak and can no longer perform at peak levels, it goes into a cave, grinds its talons and beak down to the nub, and plucks all of its feathers out. It is said that one can then hear the eagle crying throughout the canyons. The eagle remains in the dark cave without food until the talons, beak, and feathers grow back. The eagle emerges renewed. While I did not choose the pain over the last five years, I do feel that I was called into the renewing of my body, mind, emotions, and soul.

The healing process requires waiting and walking into and through the pain before transformation occurs. Each of the stories of my life bears witness to this as the pathway that life presented. I had spent much energy running from the obvious and running into brick walls emotionally and physically. Waiting is an active word. It includes preparing, not just sitting passively. It includes having an expectation that something will occur. It includes facing the pain and the courage to face what is found there.

Remaining connected to the Holy Spirit is essential for guidance and renewal. Without this guidance, we lose our way in the storms of life. Acceptance of life and the path given to us is a theme not only seen in the eagle, but we also find it in *The Lord of The Rings: The Fellowship of the Ring* when Gandalf and Frodo are talking: (I paraphrase from what I remember the words to be.)

Frodo: "I wish the ring had never come to me. I wish none of this had happened."

Gandalf: "So do all who live to see such times. But that is not for them to decide. All we have to decide is what to do with the time that is given to us. There are other forces at work, Frodo, than the will of evil. Bilbo was meant to find the ring. In which case you also were meant to have it, and that is an encouraging thought."

I believe that we are all called into a journey. We may be asked to leave behind everything we have grown dependent upon. We may be asked to bear an incredible burden. We may be given a responsibility that is beyond our experience. We may be diagnosed with a chronic or incurable disease. Eventually the strain of constantly living with whatever it is can cause one to "wish that the burden had never come upon him or her." We find this in Frodo as well as in the Old Testament profits. Moses wanted another mission. Jonah wanted to avoid his calling. Peter and James wanted to stay on their mountaintop and avoid the work of life. Jesus accepted His mission and yet, He did not want to suffer the physical pain of the crucifixion or the emotional agony of abandonment by God his father.

How are the Garden of Gethsemane and Jesus' cry to God to take his cup from him and Frodo's wishing that he did not have to carry the ring alike? How is your life similar? What in your life has become a burden?

To come to the acceptance of the life that I have been given has been a major theme in my life. I have come to realize that I have fought against God almost every step of the way. Every journey I took away from God in all of my struggles to find relief, He found me and reached out to me offering comfort and healing. God has been faithful to His promise that He will never forsake me. He has always been faithful to finish the work that He began in me.

15

THE COST OF HELPING OTHERS

My role in the family had at times been difficult to fulfill. Love required that I make hard choices. These choices were many times not easy or comfortable. Taking the easy way out would have been to do nothing. Insisting that Dad go to a center for alcohol abuse, escorting him there, testifying to his need to be in a psychiatric hospital, and telling Mother that her cancer was so advanced that her life was nearing her end were all heart wrenching conversations that the family gave to me to bear.

The kind of love that I am referring to has to do with the mind and why I decided what I did. For me love is not simply an emotion that rises unbidden in my heart. It is more of a principle by which I deliberately live. I found that throughout my life, love has called me to longsuffering, to show kindness, purged me of jealousy and encouraged me to not seek my own way. Love called me to do what was right and moral in spite of what was comfortable.

Martha's health brought me to another crossroads of love. In the summer and again in the fall of 2003, her multiple sclerosis reached a critical phase. Her judgment had been compromised because she was disoriented as a result of medical problems. One of Martha's friends and Martha's caregiver called me asking for help with her situation. This was a difficult choice for me to make since Martha did not trust that my intentions were for her best interest. She was suspicious of my intent for her intervention. She continued to believe all I wanted to do was to put her in a nursing home. Because of my love for her, I went to her home both times to talk to her about medical intervention. We discussed that a visit to the doctor was critical. She refused to go. My intervention rejected, I returned home.

In January 2004, her symptoms reached an even more critical level. Martha was seeing and hearing things and people that no one else witnessed. She had become more suspicious about other people's intentions and she exhibited bizarre behaviors in response to her suspicions. Martha owned a handgun, which she kept under her pillow at night. Her caregiver reported to me that she had put Martha's gun away for safety reasons. During one of her confused states, Martha asked for her gun. The caregiver refused. Martha got very agitated and demanded her gun. The caregiver handed the loaded gun to my sister! Martha had at one time been able to shoot the gun with precision. Because of her mental state that day, she believed that she still could. In front of the caregiver, she opened the chamber of the gun and let what she thought were all of the bullets drop to her lap. She closed the chamber, professing that she knew about gun safety. The caregiver believed that she saw one bullet still in the chamber and began to scream. Martha believed the chamber was empty and the caregiver was just being melodramatic. Martha continued to profess she knew about gun safety. She pointed the gun to her stomach and, with the caregiver still screaming, Martha pulled the trigger.

"See, there are no bullets," she demanded.

The caregiver, because she believed there was still a bullet in the chamber, was frightened to take the gun from my sister for fear of being shot. Martha was agitated now, so she put the gun to her head and, with the caregiver hysterically screaming, pulled the trigger again. Martha was certain about her judgment and she knew that the chamber was void of any bullets, or was it?

After the gun incident, her caregiver, her friend, and other professionals whom Martha did business with all called me for immediate help. I went again. Martha needed to see a physician to be evaluated, and medications prescribed for the confusion that she was having. There was possibly a medical reason unrelated to MS that could explain why she was so sick. Martha believed in combining conventional prescription medications with complementary and alternative medicines to relieve her discomfort. Without a doctor monitoring such choices (there was no practitioner of alternative medicine in her town), there was no way to know if these medicines were in conflict with one another. It was suspected that she was unaware of how much medication she was taking or when she last took what.

I drove to Martha's town and was able to make for her and take her to the doctor's appointment. After being evaluated by the doctor, she was put on medication for a horrific bladder infection and medication that would clear the confusion. The doctor instructed the caregivers to administer Martha's medication only as prescribed and in the correct dosage. Because of her confused state of mind, her condition now required that twenty-four hour care be in her home. Before I returned to my hometown, I arranged for extra help to be with her during the late night shift. With the gun out of reach, my sister properly medicated and the extra help secured, I felt it was safe for me to return home. However, I was no sooner in the door to my apartment than the phone rang. Martha's long-time caregivers were refusing to work with the new caregiver because their shifts would have to change. The old caregivers would not compromise and without any authority to make them work different hours, I had to let the new caregiver go. The original caregivers planned to provide twenty-four-hour coverage for Martha. They too, had to sleep. Who was watching my sister in her delirious state while they were asleep on the job? Believing the new medicine was actually making Martha's symptoms worse, one of the caregivers arranged for the medication to be discontinued. I did not have power of attorney for my sister. I did not even know if she had designated anyone for that responsibility. If she had, that person had not stepped up to make the decisions that would have made an impact on Martha's care.

I decided to return to Martha's home. On my way back, I drove to the home of one of her close friends to ask for his help. I thought that perhaps he could talk her into accepting continued medical intervention and the twenty-four hour care. He listened to me with what appeared to be genuine compassion. He agreed to call and talk to her.

Nothing seemed to change and my frustration just increased. I kept running into dead ends as I attempted to execute the different facets for intervention. I felt helpless to secure the help she needed to recover from this illness. Love means action leading to intervention.

Because the extra healthcare worker did not work out, I remained in Martha's home for the next two weeks. In order to help her get the care she needed during critical outbursts, I determined that calling 911 was our best option. However, the emergency team could not do anything since my sister's right to refuse medical treatment was honored. I understood the reasons why the emergency team would not take her to the hospital. She did have the right to refuse. However, she was so seriously ill. Even though she was delirious, she was still given the authority to say "no" to medical intervention. I was running into dead ends in my attempts to get her help.

Many nights, it would take two of us to keep her safe. Martha would be up all night screaming, because of things that she saw or heard. I saw the fright in her eyes as she truly experienced these thoughts and visions as her reality. I was torn apart watching her go through these horrific experiences.

Since she had become a danger to herself, I decided to have her committed to a psychiatric hospital for medical intervention, for her safety and to receive the twenty-four-hour care that she needed. Had I had the authority to change the situation at her home, or if her power of attorney had chosen to intervene, one of us would have been able to arrange the care that she needed, leaving her in the comfort of her own home or, admitting her to a medical hospital.

I did not want to commit her to a psychiatric hospital. I had been down that road with Dad and I knew the pain both Martha and I would experience. I could still see my dad's face as he asked, "You, too?" My heart was torn apart as I considered that there was no other way Martha could be protected. Doing nothing would be cruel. I loved Martha, and protection of her safety and medical intervention were necessary to bring back the Martha I knew and to help restore the quality of her life.

The process of having Martha committed to a psychiatric hospital was difficult, to say the least. This was no easy decision for me. I grieved. I had to risk that she would not understand and might never speak to me again when she returned to normal thinking. My love for her compelled me to do what I believed was right for her. Many of the procedures for admission to a psychiatric hospital had changed since Dad had been committed. Because I did not have power of attorney, my intentions were challenged every step of the way. I understood that there were laws in place to protect any individual from abuse by family members, but it was obvious my sister was sick. Once committed, the next step was for me to put into action legal requirements that mandated her having to stay until her medication could be stabilized. Martha was horrified I had signed the emergency commitment papers that required her to stay for a week of psychiatric treatment. She did not remember her behaviors while psychotic. She truly believed I had made up everything.

Martha uses an electric wheelchair. Her pushchair is small and only used when it was impossible to use her electric chair. The hospital would not allow her the option of using her electric chair. This was an extra burden on her since her independence was further removed from her. The push-wheel-chair was so very uncomfortable. Her legs would cramp often, and she had no way of reaching them to massage out the cramps. The hospital had limited sympathy for her comfort. Once her medical condition was stabilized, Martha was discharged. The entire hospital experience, from admission to discharge was a nightmare for both of us.

Based on the counsel I sought from other professionals, I faced the difficult decision of whether to file for guardianship of Martha. This was one of the most difficult decisions that I have ever had to make. The state of confusion that she was experiencing might go away, never to return. Putting Martha through the emotional and physical stress of the legal procedures might possibly increase her symptoms. I did not want to cause her more discomfort. Yet, leaving her to remain ill was not a decision that love could make. I also remembered the discussion that my mother and I had before her death. Because of Mother's understanding about Martha's medical situation, she believed that Martha's symptoms would return and therefore she had asked me to protect Martha when needed. My heart continued to be ripped apart because I knew she would possibly never understand. She had always been so independent, she had the power to make her own investments, and she ran the decisions of her life. There were two decisions before me: whether I should file and who would be the designated guardian. Maybe I should have just left things alone and walked away, leaving her to the life that she had. I loved my sister. I decided that I could not leave her as she was. I decided to file for guardianship.

By the time the scheduled court hearing came, Martha's medication was working, and she was not actively hallucinating. I had gone into the courtroom believing that the truth would be exposed and that my sister's best interest for her health would prevail. However, because of the very brief testimony that was allowed, I was not confident that Martha's situation was evaluated for her best long-term health.

The friend who had first called me for help was in the courtroom, but to testify on behalf of Martha, thus changed her original story. Another of my sister's friends called me to say that while she believed what I was doing was the correct decision, she would be in the courtroom on behalf of Martha. The caregiver who had called me initially for help was indecisive in her testimony. I felt betrayed by all of them.

The judge asked me why I should be appointed guardian. As a professional psychotherapist with experience in mental health issues, long-term disabilities, chronic illnesses and hospice care, and as a supervisor of several departments and programs, I felt very qualified to be her guardian. I also believed that I, as her sister, had a deeply bonded involvement and commitment to seek for her what would be best.

I remember the physician testified that my sister needed a guardian. He stated that due to her current medical situation her judgment and capacity to reason were impaired and that, if left to make her own decisions about her medications, she would not make healthy choices. He felt that would result in another state of confusion. Because the psychiatrist who evaluated my sister stated in court she was competent at the time he evaluated her, the judge denied my request to be guardian. The court-appointed lawyer, who had also spent additional time interviewing Martha, suggested to the judge Martha be observed for several months following the hearing to monitor her medical status. Because of the recent exacerbation of her illness, he believed it was prudent for the court to continue involvement. My lawyer agreed with the court-appointed lawyer. Martha's lawyer did not agree, nor did the judge. The monitoring of her health and needed trips to the doctor were also denied.

I did not have a burning desire to be Martha's guardian. I wanted her to be safe. It was disappointing, since I believe Martha would remain at risk. The legal system is in place to protect, but at what cost to the needs of the individual? I believed that, with my knowledge of the situation, the history of all the previous exacerbations, my love for Martha and my concern for her welfare, I had acted in good faith and in her best interest.

As I drove home after the hearing, I felt as though I had been tossed about in a violent storm. My body shook all over. I felt beaten and whipped. I felt empty. It was necessary for me to stop several times, as I was physically sick to my stomach. I was wounded by the betrayal of friends. I had been disillusioned by the court process. I was discredited as to my intent and love for my sister. And I was saddened by the wounds all of the last few months had on our sisterhood. Love asked of me to intervene then, and may in the future ask again. My worn and tattered emotions feel like saying "No way. Not again!" But the power of love is greater than any other emotion.

Picking up the pieces was strenuous. Martha came away from the court hearing believing that my actions had been a direct attempt to take away her independence and her money. She made sure everyone she knew believed my objective was to harm her. My honest intent had been to protect her from herself when confused and from others who would take advantage of her situation. She remained angry with me for many months. If I were in her shoes, I, too, would feel wounded. Knowing that she will probably never understand was a sadness that remained buried deep within my heart.

As a child, I wanted to be like her: pretty, witty, and scholastic. I envied her ability to express herself with verbal expression or the written word. I followed her around anywhere. I felt that she was confident and I harbored the feelings of inadequacy. She was popular. She was a leader and business-woman in her community. Today I admire her courage and stamina in the face of multiple sclerosis.

I had no idea how Martha was doing between our conversations. Even when we did talk, I was never sure she reported the truth. I was suspect that she was telling me what she wanted me to hear. That way she could rest easy knowing that I would not attempt to file for guardianship again. I also believe that she wanted to present an image of herself that had a resemblance of a normal life. She did remain clear minded and physically void of any serious infections that might again precipitate a state of confusion.

I do not know what I will do if she again becomes confused and no one comes forward. I began protecting her when we were children as we were about to be attacked by our Dad's mean bull. Has it come time for me to put down that role and that responsibility? How many times do I put myself in the line of fire? When does helping her, or anyone for that matter, destroy me? If I am destroyed, can I help the others in my family and community who need me?

I hope and pray Martha is, and will continue to be, surrounded by those who love her for who she is. I remain in prayer that somehow the wounds in our relationship will be healed.

As with previous relationships, it has been paramount that I evaluate my role and finish with new understanding, compassion, and forgiveness. The first issue I delved into was to look again into my motive for stepping into her life to help her. What was the difference between co-dependency and true Christian compassion for me? Co-dependency to me has a selfish root in that I am helping others in order to relieve my pain. I believe Christian compassion is the selfless giving because of the love I have for God and for another person and because I am called to do so by the one great Love. After serious introspection, I was confident the motive was because I love Martha. I was also confident I was following my Christian commitment to love one another.

The second issue I will mention here is the one that I incurred from the misunderstanding that arose between Martha and I about my intentions to protect her. The after effects were different with Dad after his commitment. His heart was broken but I knew he never stopped loving me. He had not turned away from our relationship. With Martha, it was so different that I questioned if we were to enjoy sisterhood ever again.

Pondering about those misunderstandings, I am reminded Martha is fearful of what her future holds. Fear in her life has created responses to that fear. Pushing me away even before I had offered assistance served to protect her from her fear that I might at some point, decide to put her in a nursing home. I believe fear kept her from accepting that I actually shared her same desire to make sure everything possible was done in order that she could live in her own home, whatever her medical condition. Fear in my life has forced me to behave in ways that hurt others and myself. I too spent many years covering up for my weaknesses. I would pretend that everything was all right, smile, and say all was fine. I too had a fear of the future. I also have manipulated my environment to protect my image and myself. Like her, I have verbally described my life as a picture other than the reality of what was true. I share with her times I have felt helpless and pushed people away who wanted to assist. We share the emotional scars from physical disabilities. While she chose to exaggerate my intentions as her way of power and of pushing people away, I chose avoidance. I am one with her and all others who fear the future because of an emotional, physical, or medical condition.

16

A GRATEFUL SPIRIT

Life was running rather smoothly. I thought my body was indefatigable now that my hip was healed. I forgot I had aged considerably. It seemed now that my life had calmed down, my body stopped pushing to hold together under all its stresses. Once I stopped pushing, my body fell apart in a different way. In 2005, I started to have chest pressure and difficulty breathing. I had a difficult time picking up my legs to walk. I felt heavy and was exhausted all the time. I went to the doctor and discovered that I had developed high blood pressure. After running some blood tests, He discovered that my cholesterol was high, and he put me on a diet. He prescribed exercise to increase the blood flow and increase nutrition to the brain. I had not been able to exercise for the former five years due to the pain in my hip. Now I could. With the increased exercise, I began to experience darting pains that moved from one place to another without any pattern. This new type of pain surprised me. I was tired of hurting and I had hoped to be rid of it for a while. My doctor sent me to a rheumatology specialist who diagnosed my "body pain" as arthritis. Medicine for blood pressure, high cholesterol, and arthritis were prescribed. I had to get a bigger pillbox!

More changes! I was tired of changes. I discovered that for self-preservation, I had become set in my ways and I did not want to change. My life had been out of my control for so many years and I had only recently been able to restructure my life with some sense of predictability and independence. I wanted to have quality in my life, so I began the recommended program of medications, diet and exercise. At the next visit to the doctor, he discovered that I had a mass in my abdomen. When the doctor told me the diagnosis, I felt sick in my stomach. I asked the doctor what it might be and he said that he suspected a reoccurrence of endometriosis from many years ago, but the he would not know until a sonogram was performed. It took great effort to keep from focusing on the worst possible scenario or crying in the office. All the way home, I felt so alone in my fears. Some things just do not seem to quit.

I had many questions and fears emerge in the time between being told there was a problem and not knowing what to call *it*. I thought I was going to be able to handle my fears just in my own prayer time. But the Sunday before the Monday I was to receive the prognosis from the blood work and the sonogram, I realized I was unable to find peace. I had attempted to pray my fears away—I had given my fears to Jesus hundreds of times—and then the fears would jump back into my consciousness. I had a mass in my pelvic region, and I was *scared* beyond words.

Waiting to go to the doctor to get the results tested my pride, my faith, and my ability to accept life. It tested my ability to reach out to others. It shook my very foundation all over again. I was reminded that life is *still* an ongoing journey. There are many calm times. There are many challenging times, and there are many times, when in the depths of agony, there is the blessedness of growth. The solution to this current situation might be simple. Nevertheless, the negative kept jumping into my mind and it wandered all the way to the extreme. My body began to shake with fear. In pride, I did not choose to call any of my friends to ask for prayer. The very essence of life is not a guarantee. I realized I still had some spiritual work to do.

In an Episcopal church that I had previously attended, the minister gave as a special blessing in the Eucharist service a portion of the priest's host bread to any member of the congregation who had a special need. I believed this practice was a ritual all Episcopal ministers did. I have since come to understand that is not the case. However, on this particular day, I believed the minister had special reasons why he chose to give a portion from the priest's host bread (the communion wafer used during the initial portion of the euchristic liturgy).

After entering the church, on this day, I knelt in prayer. I surrendered my future once again to God for His will to be done. I asked for the reassurance that He would be there no matter what the outcome of the test results. I asked that the minister would be led by the Holy Spirit to give to me a special portion from the priest's host at the communion table as my way of knowing that my prayers were heard. When it was time for communion, I went forward. I was kneeling at the altar rail with my hands out stretched, and the minister placed in them a special portion from the priest's host. Peace washed over me, and I was full. It was if I heard God say I am with you *always.* I was void of fear about the surgery or the outcome from that moment.

I went into surgery confident God was with me. My emotions were no longer focused on fear of dying or of having cancer. They had shifted to remaining in union with the God who loves me. The tumor turned out to be of benign substance. There were no complications from surgery and recovery was rapid.

Why was this surgery easy when it took three surgeries to fix my hip? I have no idea. God heals in His way, in His order and in His time. One of the things that I have found was that God healed me according to His priorities, not mine. I have found that He repeatedly puts spiritual healing first. Just as God's healings were operative in my transformation, it was necessary for the obstacles, which hindered me from the transformation, to be removed. What lessons did I carry with me into this crisis this time? I was given a grateful spirit. I accepted a willingness to accept. I was able to let go of pride. With God's help, I could walk into another valley, with assurance God was there to walk the path with me no matter what.

I mentioned before, I had no idea how God would work out the healing between my sister and me. A month after surgery and two years after Martha's court case, Hurricane Rita was about to roll through Texas and my sister needed a place to go. After several invitations, she reluctantly left her home and came to mine. That crisis in her life gave us a chance to repair sisterhood. I am grateful my sister was able to come to my home for such a long visit. It gave us both an opportunity to get to know one another again and to allow the healing opportunities to begin.

Having Martha in my home for three weeks gave me further understanding of the needs and challenges primary caregivers have to face.

There were many challenges for me in the caregiver role. Sometimes it was difficult to maintain proper boundaries between my sister and myself. If my boundaries became lost, then identity was lost. I sometimes exposed myself to repeated and prolonged stress without any relief. (see Appendix F). I had to make sure I kept my social support active. We had to make sure we both maintained an attitude of respect for one another. We both had to work on not imposing upon the other. We finally had an opportunity to enjoy one another, and it was important for both of us to remain positive and to communicate. By grace, we were able to rebuild our estranged sisterhood.

Given that the transitions of my life have been ever-changing, I am certain that elderhood will not be any different. I have already begun the evaluation of the questions: "What do I want to do with the time that is left?" And "How do I want to live with quality and meaning in the future?" I have begun to downsize and give away possessions that seem to be in the way. I am surrounding myself only with things that bring me joy. If I am not using "it," it is no longer in my possession. I used to have five storage sheds of memories and now I have reduced the clutter. I am interested in many hours of quiet time. My body and energy levels are slowing down. I choose what I want to do rather than what others want me to do. I seek quality rather than quantity. I do maintain my group of close friends and I do have ways I serve in my community. I continue to offer professional psychotherapy, spiritual direction, and pastoral assistance on a limited basis.

I read, exercise, get sunshine, and attempt to stay on a heart-healthy diet (which is not easy for me). It is important to me to keep an active mind, nurture my ability to be flexible and strive for a positive outlook. Staying involved will help to keep me young and live longer. Fifty-nine plus is a time when I need to do what I can to maintain a healthy lifestyle. I am learning that no matter what happens to my body, my quality of life is not dependent on my health. I also am learning that any illness I might incur is not my identity. The way I take care of my body will allow me to have a longer life to enjoy.

Even though I am in the senior years, I have a life of experiences to share. I also believe I still have much to learn about life and myself. I hope the quest never ends. I look forward to continued learning and continued sharing with others. My spiritual quest for the God I love continues to pull me into an even deeper relationship with Him.

As with any relationship, the more you get to know someone that you love, the more you want to know about him or her. My love for God is no different. I have only just begun to walk the spiritual walk. I will continue to reach deep within to search for the Truth. I think that I am going to like growing older. I have gained great wisdom from life that could not have been gained through textbooks.

Moving into my senior years will continue to be an adventure for me. I am relying on these latter years to be the richest ever in my spiritual growth with increased wisdom gained through the living of my life. The more I have learned, the more I realize I do not know much about anything. I have just begun to learn. I hunger for more of life and the gifts that are offered to me.

Looking back on a prayer that was beside my mother's bed, which I have now adopted as one of my own, I find that the words speak to the very essence of my life with my loving creator and healer:

I asked for strength that I might achieve
I was made weak that I might obey
I asked for health that I might do greater things
I was given infirmity that I might do better things
I asked for riches that I might be happy
I was given poverty that I might be wise
I asked for Power that I might have the praise of men
I was given weakness that I might feel the need of God
I asked for all things that I might enjoy life
I was given life that I might enjoy all things
I have nothing that I asked for but everything I hoped for
My prayers *are* answered
I am most blessed.
—Anonymous

17

PUTTING IT ALL TOGETHER

Not all of my life was consumed with struggles or pain. I have had many wonderful experiences that have also brought about transformation. The sight of a breath-taking sunset or rainbow, for example, has the power to fill my soul with wonder. Wonder is healing. Nature is able to communicate life and the gift of life that we have been given. Taste, touch, smell, and sight all enable me to experience life in a mystical way. I am more than flesh and blood.

As I have mentioned, our family returned to the same place every year for a vacation. We were able to take side trips into the mountains, and healing came when I was there. Yearly, I would feel renewed as I would smell the mountain air and see the strength that the mountains would express. I sensed the family was in harmony with one another. The mountains had running streams from freshly melted snow. I loved to wade in the water even though it was cold. The running streams would bring me comfort and renewal. The every-day cares of life were postponed for a month. For me, mountains are where God lives. They appear so strong and powerful. They have a presence of having been there for a long time, and I know the next time I return, they will still remain.

Humor was healing. Laughter in relationships, but not laughing at someone else, was healing. Merriment in dancing or gatherings (I am not referring to a party that has mind altering drugs or alcohol) brought healing. Appreciation for the arts in all forms brought healing. Appreciation was healing. Joy was healing. Developing and maintaining a joyful spirit was healing. Gratitude for everything in life was healing. Forgiveness heals across time. Wonderment restored the child within. A deep abiding faith and belief in something greater than myself helped to bring security and an awareness of who I was created to be. Time out was healing, too, for a break brought me back to my center. It was necessary for me to take a yearly vacation to a place I yearned to go. Time out also included reading a good book or meditation time. The point of the time out was to establish once again who was in control of my life and to withdraw from the demands of life and others. Spontaneous play was healing. Being creative was healing. Risking my boundaries to adventure into something I had always wanted to do but was afraid to do was healing.

It did not matter what modality was used to bring about transformation in my life. They all came from the same guiding source. I was surprised that I was given such a variety of paths. God has given me the ability to see Him in all things and in all people. He has shown me I can find Him anywhere. He has taught me the focus of my life *is* to seek Him. He has proved He is faithful in all of my circumstances and has never abandoned His love or intervention for me. He has spoken to me through every event recorded in this book.

My transformation process required a serious look into the physical, psychological, and spiritual dimensions of my life. In the transitions my life advanced through, I moved differently on those three plains, yet they overlapped each other. Physically, I evolved from conception to seniorhood. My body has changed shape, and I have experienced the aging process. My body has absorbed all the stresses as my front line of defense. The body has memory and remembers everything. The "body memory" asked for healing as well. It has worn down several times and was in need of medical intervention. Because of the body's natural ability to heal, it recovered successfully.

Psychologically, I moved from abandonment, insecurity, low self-esteem, worthlessness, anxiety, rage, inadequacy in handling a situations, loneliness, helplessness in the victim role, shame and mistrust to personal boundaries, healthy self-appraisal, authority, a sense of connection, competency, willingness to communicate and to the forgiveness of others and self.

"Father forgive them; for they know not what they do." (Luke 23:34, RSV) are the recorded words of Jesus from the cross. I have given several examples of how forgiving someone who hurt me because I believed that they were remorseful brought healing in my heart. I have also given examples of how forgiving others even though they had no remorse for their hurts also healed me. In rage or resentfulness against another, I believe there is a powerful chemical that is released into the system. This chemical can begin to destroy the body. When I have held resentment, I have experienced headaches, digestive disorders, and heart trouble, to name a few. The person responsible for the hurt generally did not experience the damaging chemical change because of his or her actions. I have observed a strange phenomenon relating to forgiveness. The phenomenon was apparent when I had been hurt by someone who would not ask for forgiveness but I chose to forgive that person anyway. The reason to forgive is because "they do not know what they do" in the overall plan of life. It is not condoning what they did. Nor is it negating the hurtfulness of the actions. Forgiveness is bigger than that. It is related to truly believing that the person does not understand how his or her actions or words affect others, the earth, and even onward out into the universe. When forgiveness is given, there sets in motion a release of energy for both persons. If unforgiveness continues, the other person can justify his or her stance and be unwilling to face the consequences of his or her actions. Unforgiveness then actually helps the other person to continue to hurt others and to maintain blindness to his or her hurtful actions, never reaching an awareness of what he or she did and thus having no desire to ask for forgiveness.

Another reason I chose to forgive was the honest understanding that I have hurt others by my words and deeds even though I may not have hurt others in the same way that I was hurt. To be able to realistically look into my own life and evaluate my motives, words and actions enabled me to forgive others.

I went through a period of time in which I found I could not forgive God for what I believed were cruel and unnecessary situations. I went into a depth of rage. I cursed the day I was born before I came to understand God is aware and He had a magnificent plan for my life. It was humbling to face just how little I really know about God's plan for me.

The hardest of all to forgive is myself. I could accept my forgiveness of others and my forgiveness from God, even accept that others would never forgive me. It was my forgiving myself I found difficult. I held on to the idea, that if I did not forgive myself, somehow I could retain the power to erase or change the situation. Maybe it was pride. Whatever the reasons, I found it difficult to forgive myself and to accept myself as a whole human being, perfectly imperfect.

I discovered a repetitive pattern: the things that almost destroyed me were the very things that set me free. Gifts in life were showered upon me in spite of all the struggles. I had previously lived emotionally frightened that I would be destroyed by events and the words of others. The emotional structure of my life was rebuilt to sustain me in most all situations. All the challenges and all of the gifts either reinforced or awakened my yearning to search for the truth and to be set free from the past that had kept me in bondage and from discovering and becoming the person that I was created to be.

Spiritually, my understanding of God grew deeper, wider and with more awe for His loving presence. I have moved from my will in stubbornness or fear to surrender. Looking back over my life at the development of my faith, I discovered patterns of movement and patterns of resistance to change. Each stage provided substance for transformation to the next. The more I deliberately chose to let God direct my every thought, word and action, the more profoundly my life with Him was affected. God called me continually to recognize Him in my life and to respond.

I began as a child of faith ready to accept anything having to do with God. I believed unconditionally the faith stories. Faith was simple. I talked to God, and He answered all of my dialogues. I believed He was omnipotent. I believed He intervened in my life. I believed He would provide what I needed. God was my best friend and Father/Mother. I identified with the Bible stories. As an adopted child, I formed a belief my life was similar to the life of Moses in that I was of genetic making from one family and, for God's reasons, I was raised in another. I believed and did not need to question. My self-concept of worthlessness, shame and guilt as well as mistrust of others hindered my growth until early adulthood. My body concept, the overbearing limp, the pain, and the social stigma related to having dyslexia reinforced my negative self-image. The crisis of fearing that the tumor I had was going to kill me was the impetus that sparked my growth to the next level of spiritual development.

With the revelation of the Light of Christ, I moved into service, knowledge and steadfastness in the witness to God as seen in Jesus Christ. I was busily serving in the church and verbally witnessing to the truth as it had been revealed to me. I was almost too heavenly to be of any use on earth. I had a profound sense that I was loved and called to be a disciple. However, I was timid about allowing God to have His way with my emotions. I kept finding excuses to hold on to the negative self-esteem. It took alcoholism to shake me loose from holding so tightly to the past.

Recovering from alcoholism sent me into the depths of this person was who was created in the image of God. Accepting my heritage as a child of God was a gift from God Himself. I felt the presence of the Holy Spirit leading me into self-discovery in a way that was painful. Had I known beforehand that I would be put in the furnace to burn away the chaff, I might not have gone.

When physical pain returned into my life, I turned and ran from the gift of intimate friendship that God was offering. I began to question why He was allowing me to hurt. I lost the patience of my youth to endure. I found myself in a spiritual crisis like no other time in my life. I questioned the omnipotent power of God. I questioned if God answers prayers for some and not others.

Self-realization can be scary and is very painful. I felt the burden of hurting so many people. I was asked to see clearly my responsibility for my actions. It was difficult to separate the spiritual healing in this phase from the psychological. God was offering me wholeness and not dividing me into specific sections. As the psychological side of me was in the process of healing, so was the spiritual and vice versa. A loving hand guided me in word and in deeds. In spite of all my own effort, God brought me through the furnace to the side of illumination. I was beginning to embrace my humanity. I was beginning to forgive myself for things I had done and things I had left undone that God had given to me to do. I began to see the talents I had been given that I had wasted. I was not the one who orchestrated the events or insights that brought me safely to the next level of understanding. I was aware God was calling me, and all I had to do was respond to His leading. I began to relinquish more of my life and my will in obedience to God. The more I gave to Him; the more He blessed me with Himself.

Once illuminated, I was surprised to discover that there is so much more. The God I had known was outgrowing my limited understanding of Him. He showered me with dreams and symbols as teaching tools. I began to realize I really knew nothing at all about God. I had witnessed the Light of Christ, the ongoing power of the Holy Spirit and the assurance that God was the same God throughout all history, but I knew nothing really. My desire to engage in an intimate relationship with God became a hunger I could not satisfy. I began classes in spiritual direction; I immersed myself in more Bible study, and joined a group that was exploring spirituality. I was filled with the desire to disconnect from the ties and attachments of this world. My lifestyle changed to include more solitude and less clutter. I was learning rapidly that God is in all but that even the "all" does not define God. The closer I moved to God, the more He revealed to me and the more I realized how little I really knew.

Psychologically, I was called to another level of letting go of the ties that had kept me locked into the past. I spent much time trying to initiate the answers. I wore myself out striving to make my life less painful. Seeking therapy again opened the doors for psychological and spiritual transformation. I call that period of growth a "dark night of my soul" because I felt withered and alone. I searched but did not find. I grieved but still felt that I was losing. I felt alone and thought that God had abandoned me. I was being called to relinquish something in my identity. Giving it up did not mean losing although it felt like it at the time. It did mean to detach from whatever was preventing me from walking humbly and obediently with God. He was providing all the open doors for me to walk through. He was holding the candle in the darkness. I was over in the corner complaining about my pain and that no one cared about me. Oh, how wonderful and gracious God is. He faithfully held on to me. He did not abandon me, even though I turned and ran. The realization that He has always been with me no matter where I went or how I got there brought me to my knees, and not just literally.

Spiritually, I came to see a loving guide and friend. I do not have any answers for why I was allowed to hurt for so long, or why He seems to answer some prayers and why He waits to answer others. I do not yet even have a way of describing God. He remains to be seen through a mist and only experienced as an elusive presence. Spiritual growth for me has only begun.

18

STORIES FROM THE OTHER CHAIR

My professional career as a psychotherapist and spiritual director has brought many challenges and rewards. I have heard stories that would break your heart and stories that bring celebration. In this chapter I will give several examples from the other chair in my therapy room to further show how difficult it is not only to begin the search but also to continue the lifetime search for wholeness. There are several reasons why people come to therapy: To get an immediate situation resolved; to resolve the situation and to prevent it from occurring again; to resolve a situation, to prevent it from occurring again and to explore other issues that might be interfering with the journey toward wholeness; and to seek God's direction. Only a few persons stay in therapy or spiritual direction until they reach a sense of completion. Life is ongoing, and so is the healing process.

I have found that all people who have shared their stories with me are searching for answers to such questions as: Who am I? Why am I here? Why is this happening to me? Where do I go from here? How do I cope? How can we get along together? I would like to share a few stories with you now, as told to me by others, as examples of our human condition.

Will's story

Will came to my office because he was suffering with anxiety. He shared with me his story about his family of origin and how his father was rather violent. As he described his intense hatred for his father, his face became red and his breathing increased. He raged as he blamed his father for all of his life problems. He blamed his father for the way he was coping with life now. He was supersensitive and very self-absorbed. As a defense against feeling out of control, he had learned to manipulate others to get what he wanted. He shared that he knew how to move into someone's emotions and attack him or her there. He knew he had power over them at that point. If that did not work, then he would become physically violent. He was unwilling to relinquish one form of power to learn another. His concept of power did not include compromise, debate, the possibility of not getting what he wanted or personal responsibility. We discussed why he was in therapy and he came to the decision that, if he had to change his manipulative behaviors in any way to reduce his anxiety, he would not change. At that point in his life he was not willing to go through the uncertainty and chaos necessary to resolve the issues, nor was he willing to take responsibility for his own life's choices. He chose to keep his rage and his cruel manipulation, even if it cost him a high level of anxiety. He did not return to therapy.

Ann's story

Ann came to talk with me because she was not able to adjust to a new medical diagnosis. She spent much of the initial session giving examples about how her body was giving way. She had been for several consultations in seeking a different diagnosis. It is a normal reaction to resist a lifestyle-altering diagnosis. There is usually a period of denial, of anger or resistance, of seeking many other opinions, of bargaining with something greater than oneself, of depression and then hopefully of learning to live with the situation. Each session, we were processing the same issue: she did not want to be sick and she was just plain angry. The angrier she got the sicker she got. Transferring her to a medical doctor for an anti-depressant was her best solution. Therapy could not make the external situation go away, and that was her goal for coming.

Hank's story

Hank came to my office because of prescription abuse. He just wanted to stop his drug pattern of addiction. We discussed his history of drug abuse. We discussed drug relapse prevention, which would require changes that would be permanent. He began to do the work required. He began to identify patterns of emotions and responses. He began to risk taking responsibility for his thoughts, feelings, and beliefs. As we began to delve into his caretaking role and how that defined his identity, he began to resist changing. As reported by a family member one afternoon after a difficult session, the client went home, curled into a fetal position on the floor in the corner of his bedroom and withdrew into a nap. The next session the client returned to therapy and announced that he would not change. He was not going to do any more work. For if he did change, he would no longer know who he was. Moving through the pain was too difficult for him at that time in his life. He has since returned to his pattern of substance abuse.

Betty's story

Betty came to my office because she wanted help from me in filing for disability with the Social Security administration. She had already been told by several doctors that she was too young to just give up on her life without learning new coping skills. She had a panic disorder, which interfered with her ability to keep a steady job. Whenever she was overcome with panic, she was unable to function. She had never learned coping skills that would help to reduce the intensity of her attacks. She was given the option to learn new skills and then to re-evaluate her need for SSDI assistance. She refused. Her goal was to remain in the role of "sick." She was getting her needs met by being ill. I never saw her again. Some people do not get well because they want the benefits that they perceive to be gained from being ill.

Anthony and Lucy's story

I had a father and his daughter come into therapy. He brought her in because she had announced to him that she had chosen the lesbian lifestyle. She stated that it had been a difficult and lonely journey into the darkest corners of her heart, but that she had come to the awareness that this was who she was. He became irate because his wish for his daughter was not her choice. He screamed at me because I could not "fix" her and ran out of the room, never to return. His daughter continued to commit to therapy, and with hard work, she developed a sense of honor and respect for herself that she had never had. She retired from therapy feeling whole. She had been restored to herself through forgiveness and true self-acceptance.

Pete's story

I visited Pete who had just been brought into the hospital because of third degree burns to his hands. He was in excruciating pain and frightened not only about being able to keep his hands but also what the future would hold for him. His hands were bandaged, and he had been given a heavy dose of medication. The medication was not reducing the pain. After he was able to let go of his macho facade and truthfully describe his fears and his vulnerability, his pain level reduced. He was able to sleep. I am convinced that his willingness to talk about his fears assisted his body in moving toward recovery. He actually recovered the full use of his hands and without any scarring.

Carol's story

As the therapist on a hospice team, I walked with a very special woman, Carol, through her journey into death. On one particular day that I visited her, she was having a crisis about the meaning of her life and her death. Much of her suffering was related to an inability to engage the deepest questions of life. She was essentially lonely because no one was there with whom to share her journey. She was living in her daughter's home but the client did not want to grieve her daughter by talking about death. She felt terror as she contemplated going through "the valley of the shadow of death" alone. I listened while she remembered her life and the events of special meaning. I listened as she shared business that was not yet finished. I listened as she defined her faith in a way that allowed questions.

After our visit, I went to a park near her home. I picked up leaves from an oak tree and maple tree. I picked up acorns as well. Fall had already come and the leaves were changing colors. The next day I took my collection to her home. We talked about the cycle of life from birth (the acorn) through the dying process (the turning leaves) and then on to death (the very dried, dark brown leaves). The acorn also symbolized that it had to separate from the life of the tree before it could seed into the ground and produce new life. She was blessed with the comfort that she needed to face her fears.

Several months later, as she was in the last few hours of her life, she told me that she was convinced we all get to have an escort into death. She told me that she had asked to be mine and that she would be back for me. She was able to face her fears in death and find peace.

Amanda and Justin's story

Amanda came to my office because she was suffering with a chronic debilitating disease. She easily fatigued all the time. Justin, her husband, was having difficulty adjusting to the lifestyle changes that she needed to make. She had been a faithful serving wife. Now he resented that he had to sometimes put his free time aside to assist her. He began to express his resentment through aggressive and abusive behaviors.

When she came into my office, she was separated, bruised, and confused. Both she and her husband eventually were able to face their concepts of the masculine and feminine roles and admit to each other their hopes for the relationship and their fears for the future. They were able to risk being vulnerable with one another, which literally set them free to embrace a meaningful relationship. Reaching that level of communication was a process. Justin stopped coming for a time but returned because he loved her more than he loved his need to be aggressive against her.

Brad's story

Brad, a Native American, come to therapy because of alcoholism and aggressive behavior. He grew up on a reservation. He and the other members had been converted through the Baptist faith. He had lost connection with his Indian roots. He had been through several rehab centers and was again back in the cycle of drinking. We focused on his realigning himself with his roots. I listened to his story about his life on the reservation. I listened to his beliefs and the grief in losing what had been passed down through many generations. Spirituality is not a set of beliefs; it is life itself. One benefit that was passed down to him was that he was to remain stoic. Yet, he was acting out his confusion in inappropriate ways. He had lost a sense of pride for himself and for his heritage.

The more we talked about his roots, the more he was able to connect. We found a rehab center that incorporated Native American traditions into his healing modality. I discharged him from my care, transferring him on to continue exploring his roots. No matter which culture is ours, there is a rich history that, when it is lost or devalued, causes a loss of identity. That young man had courage to face his nightmares and to reach out again to seek answers.

Albert's story

One of the most profound transformations that I witnessed was when I walked with Albert, a middle-aged man, who had just lost his father, his business, his marriage, and his only brother. He was bordering on depression. To maintain his ability to work, he minimized the intensity of his situation. He had the courage to face the grief of losing his father and his brother. He was able to accept his part in the destruction of the marriage while also acknowledging his wife's responsibility. He was able to face and resolve the loss of his business and his identity he associated with his losses.

Therapy was not the only way he grew. He also sought spiritual direction. He read many books relating to healing and talked with other men about the deeper meanings of life. His goal was to find peace and wholeness. It has taken him ten years to find the peace within that he was seeking. He has begun to enjoy the search for wholeness and is committed to spending the rest of his life in pursuit of that goal.

19

IT IS YOUR TURN

In the writing of this manuscript, I was surprised to have been blessed in new and different ways. New insights came together that I had not previously considered. For example, when I reread my manuscript, I discovered that I had not put the two rape experiences together or questioned what their effect on my marriage had been. I found it interesting that just prior to my marriage was date rape, and just prior to the marriage ending was, again, rape. My marriage was sandwiched in between the two rape experiences, so to speak. It became clear that because I had not processed the date rape, my ability to mature into a healthy relationship in my marriage was hindered. The effects of the date rape were far more reaching than I had actually imagined. Being able to see my life in these new ways seemed to bring form. Order was created out of chaos, and I was blessed.

I believe that each of us has a story to tell. It can be told from many different angles and at different times in one's life. It can be told about one event or about as many events as needed to communicate the point. It can be told in chronological order or very much out of order. It can be written from a physical, emotional, and/or spiritual perspective. My story was written from all three perspectives. Your story can be written from the account of what is called a genogram, or a family tree, which places the story in patterns of beliefs and values that have been passed down from one person to another and from one generation to the next. Your story can be in journal format, or in the format of a memoir, a poem, a short story, or a mystery novel. It can be autobiographical or truth disguised as fiction. The finished product can be stored under your bed, or in a safety deposit box. It can be shared with a friend, with family, or with a therapist. It can be burned or buried. The process and the insights gained will remain with you forever. Your story is not limited to writing. It can be sung, painted, sculpted, or danced. Any imaginable creative expression will allow your story to be told. I encourage you to put your life in a form for you to see and possibly to be shared with others. The healing power of this exercise is beyond your wildest dreams.

It is very important to insure that you are safe when you write. Writing tends to bring up many memories. Writing can help you to heal, but I suggest that you proceed slowly and cautiously. If you ever feel you are at risk, for example, of losing control or acting on dangerous thoughts, you should consult a qualified, professional therapist. If you are already in therapy, I suggest that you talk to your therapist about and before starting this project. I want to make it very clear here that writing your story alone is not recommended for individuals who are vulnerable to a psychotic process, to severe depression, or if you have experienced severe traumas in the past. Trained professionals should be available for those individuals.

I offer you a possible outline for writing your story:

1. Begin by writing a life timeline of your life: birth to present day.
2. Identify the main periods of your life by age, topic, or time.
3. Detail the main events of the period and the elements that make up the plot of your personal story.
4. Describe the situation and your role. What went particularly well and what special challenges did your over come? What special talents did you use?
5. Include the physical, psychological, and spiritual highs and lows of each period.
6. Describe the people in your life and your relationship to them.
7. What values were met and which were challenged or threatened?
8. Examine the major discoveries and the insights of each period or each event that has occurred as you have moved along on your journey.
9. Indicate those points where you feel that your story has been significantly bisected by the Divine story.

Living by example is a form of telling your story. Is the life that you are living the one that you desire others to know? To live by example calls one to be who and what he or she believes. It requires that one has examined one's motives, one's intent, one's values, one's behaviors, and one's words—really to evaluate everything. An unexamined life is a barren wasteland. There is much to be discovered when one risks looking within.

Our life is impossible without memory. We are not able to function effectively in the present without knowledge of who we have been in the past. The past is the womb of the future and at each moment, the present is born. The narrative of your life story is the arena in which God, through whatever means deemed necessary, "acts" to recreate you. I do believe our spiritual life cannot deepen fully outside of an awareness of our personal history.

This book has been about my life as an on going process through the painful valleys and beyond. There had to be a death before there could be a birth. There had to be a birth before there was a death. Order came from chaos. The chaos was actually necessary so that order could be formed. Nothing is considered hidden until it is known. I have become transformed as I have risked looking at situations and persisting until I embraced the rewards. I had the opportunity to revisit some of my unfinished business at later developmental stages so that my wholeness could be more complete. My life story is always a work of art in progress. As I progressed along life's journey, I continued to see miracles that opened my eyes to the wonder of who I am.

By what truths do we live? By what truths do we understand who we are? Where do we invest your energies during this brief time called life? Are we living the life that we chose, or are we living someone else's life choices for them? By what point of reference do we make your decisions? The self stands at the core of being. It is the carrier of what the soul intends. This calling to peace in the inner self will not make our life easy or free of suffering nor will it win the praises of our friends or community, but it will fill our life with meaning, purpose and a general sense of the rightness of our life's path.

Storytelling has always been at the heart of being human. I believe we have the need to pass along our traditions and our heritage. We need to confess our shortcomings and failings. We need to find healing of present or past wounds. We need to be able to bring hope to a suffering world. We need to connect with a larger community.

As a witness to another's story, I may discover that someone else has a problem similar to mine, and as I hear it or read it in another person's words, I may gain new insights into my own dilemma. Sometimes as I hear or read an individual explore possible resolution to his or her problem my own inner teacher is awakened. At the very least, knowing that someone else has a problem like mine gives me a sense of not being crazy or alone.

Because our stories make us vulnerable to others who may want to "fix" us or exploit us, or dismiss us or ignore us, we have learned to tell guardedly or not at all. Instead of telling our story, we talk about our opinions, ideas, and beliefs rather than about our lives. We discount our struggles as though they are weaknesses to hide. I am convinced that neighbors, co-workers and even family members can live side by side for years, maybe even a lifetime, without learning much about the others' lives. As a result, I believe that we lose something of great value. For in truly seeing another person, we must seek to understand his or her situation and then we are able to have a fuller understanding of ourselves.

All the tools that you need to write your story are within you. You were a witness to the events. You experienced them. You saw them happen. You felt them in your body. You have depth of emotions that go along with the events. The words are waiting for expression.

Lord, help others to remember where they have been and how You have walked the journey of life by their side. Lord, bring forth the essence of the lives of your people so that their lives and their memories will be a testimony to Your redeeming quality. My prayer for you, the reader, is that you will be blessed in the telling of your life's story. Amen.

I now invite you to begin the journey of writing your own unique story and of finding the mystery and blessings therein.

APPENDIX A

TYPES OF LOSS THAT I HAVE EXPERIENCED

Loss of:

- Control
- Freedom to travel and plan
- Security
- Productivity
- Independence and mobility
- Physical and mental skills
- Pleasures
- Sexual functioning
- Appearance
- Defined roles
- Hopes and dreams
- Social contact
- Favorite activity
- Friend
- Esteem and identity
- Source of meaning
- Possessions
- Confidence
- Pride
- Attention and recognition
- Financial resources
- Trust
- Carefreeness
- Comfort
- Hobbies
- Strength
- Routine
- Position and status
- Perspective

APPENDIX B

Whole person ideally is a balance of both masculine and feminine traits. This list was in a handout given to my spiritual direction class at The Anglican School of Theology.
Dallas, Texas. (Dr. Troy Campbell, 1999)

Masculine traits tend toward the following:

POSITIVE	NEGATIVE
Initiative talking	Intrusive, pushy
Focused	Unwilling to yield or deviate course
Linear, logical	Unimaginative
Analytic more than synthetic	Overly skeptical
Left brained	Unable to make new associations or connections
Positive energy	Negative, destructive or fragmenting force
Goal oriented	Driven to achieve
Strength of purpose	Overly-forceful
Self disciplined	Violent
Individuated	Narcissistic, ego-centered
Confident	Power hungry
Penetrating power	Entitled by force of power
Overcomer of obstacles	Heavy handed
Able to let go of old patterns, habits, traditions	Inflexible
Fearless	Grandiose
Orderly	Isolated
Successful	Cocky
Conquering	Unwilling to bond or commit
Territorial	Insensitive to other's feelings
Boundary making	Unbonded
In the head/ intellect	Over intellectual; Unfeeling/heartless
Emphasis on doing rather than being	Driven; unable to rest or be still

Feminine traits tend toward the following:

POSITIVE	NEGATIVE
Passive; receptive	Unable to use force
Diffuse	Unfocused; disorganized
Non-linear; holistic; associational	Illogical
Synthetic more than analytic	Gullible; unable to discern
Right brained	Impractical; idealistic; lost in imagine; head in the clouds
Gentle energy	Easily pushed aside
Flexible	Unable to strive for a goal
Purpose is to respond to the moment	Never able to plan ahead or set goals
Responsive; contemplative	Unable to get mind out of inwardness in order to accomplish
Bonded	Unable to separate oneself
Loving	Over-concern of others to the exclusion of self
Power to attract; receptive power	Easily intruded upon; overly seductive
Able to respond with grace to unexpected needs	Unable to push aside obstacles to stay on task
Able to form close attachments	Unable to let go of attachments; dependent; symbiotic
Sensitive to possibility of harm	Fearful
Responsive to entirety of circumstances	Disorganized
Supportive of achievements of others	Spoiling
Enjoys being swept off one's feet or conquered by love	Too easily swayed; seducible
Protective of the child	Indulgent to the child
Inclusive	Unboundaried
Lives from the heart or feeling	Sentimental; sloppy in thought
Emphasis on being rather than doing	Lazy; overly passive

APPENDIX C

Spiritual direction has a long and distinguished history in the Church. After years of neglect, this time-honored ministry has been reawakened because we all need support in order to grow up in Christ. God the Holy Spirit is, of course, the true spiritual director who relentlessly pursues His children and desires to transform them into the likeness of Christ. The spiritual director, who is the Spirit's instrument, functions as a midwife who brings forth new spiritual life. The spiritual director redirects attention from the surface events of a life toward a fuller spiritual understanding in order to cultivate growth at the soul level. The director is sensitive to the leading of the Holy Spirit in order to lead from God's will, not human will.

Spiritual direction is a highly personalized ministry that respects each individual's life history, temperament, level of maturity and vocation. Each person is unique and each journey is individualized. There is no one right way to walk with God. The director is ever challenged to hear God's call.

The goals of spiritual direction are threefold. In the realm of knowing, the spiritual director helps the directee to understand God's will as revealed in Scripture and illumined by faithful spiritual writings. In the realm of being, the director prays for the transformation of the directee's inner world after the image of Christ. In the realm of doing, the director encourages the directee to faithfully live out the gospel in the power of the Spirit.

The spiritual director assists the one seeking direction to process his/her relationship with God, to uncover resistance to growth, and to expose previously hidden pockets of sin. The director guides the practice of spiritual discipleship, facilitates listening to God and encourages a life of prayer. In short, he or she clears the interior ground of the soul and replants in it the living Word in order to nurture the release of the life of Christ from within. The spiritual director will listen, question, rephrase, suggest, offer responses, and pray with and for the one seeking direction, all the while resisting the temptation to function merely as an advisor or a problem solver.

There are trained spiritual directors in many faith traditions. Within the Christian tradition, spiritual direction is defined as the ministry of soul care in which a gifted and experienced trained Spiritual Director helps another person to grow in relationship with and obedience to God by following the example of Jesus Christ. According to Henri Nouwen, a spiritual director is not a counselor, a therapist, or an analyst, but a mature fellow Christian to whom we choose to be accountable for our spiritual life and from whom we can expect prayerful guidance in our constant struggle to discern God's active presence in our lives. (Nouwen, 2006).

Pastoral care is different from spiritual direction. The focus of pastoral care is upon the healing, guiding, supporting, reconciling, nurturing, liberating, and empowering of people in whatever situation they find themselves.

To be trained as a spiritual director and later to embark in pastoral care was a passion for me. Classes were long and the volumes of reading information seemed endless. The more I pursued my passion the more the strange phenomenon of transformation moved into my heart. The kinds of jobs that I have sought have been a reflection of my continuing transformation.

Psychotherapy is also different from spiritual direction or pastoral care. When I made the decision to become a psychotherapist, I had already determined that each person is a combination of mind, emotions, and spirit. I believe that my call into psychotherapy is a true spiritual calling, every bit as strong as those who are called into the ordained ministry. People bring to me their broken hearts, torn lives, misplaced dreams, and shame, and together we would attempt to rebuild their lives. Prayer and the guidance of the Holy Spirit lead me in all sessions. The Holy Spirit gives me insights that no book could have ever taught me. Confession in a nonjudgmental atmosphere is a miracle that occurs repeatedly. My clients reach lasting levels of healing when the spiritual areas of their lives are addressed. For many the spiritual is simply a concept of something greater than the self. The important part of the spiritual is that each person found for himself or herself what was their own belief. Healing is about the person seeking healing within.

APPENDIX D

Dr. Francine Shapiro is the founder of Eye movement, desensitization, and reprocessing known as EMDR, an information processing therapy that uses an eight-phase approach. (Shapiro, 2001).

EMDR is a complex approach to psychotherapy that combines elements from a number of therapeutic methods (among them psychodynamic, cognitive, behavioral, interpersonal, experiential, body-centered and Freudian-based therapies) in order to relieve physical and emotional complaints resulting from traumatic or upsetting experiences. It is based on the assumption that specific traumatic experiences from the past can continue to govern a person's responses in the present. These experiences can be large traumas that result in post traumatic stress disorder (PTSD), a condition characterized by sleeplessness, anxiety, and phobias, or they can be smaller traumas that are less dramatic but still negatively impact personality and behavior.

In EMDR, the client attends to past and present experiences in brief sequential doses while simultaneously focusing on an external stimulus. The client is then instructed to let new material become the focus during the next set of dual attention. This sequence of dual attention and personal association is repeated many times in the session.

EMDR works to bring traumatic memories to a positive resolution. The memories about traumatic events are stored in the memory and resurface when triggered. No one knows exactly how EMDR works and some dismiss it as "pseudoscience." Francine Shapiro, Ph.D. postulates that humans have an information processing system in the brain. While memories of an ordinary event are processed completely and normally, memories of a traumatic event may be insufficiently processed and remain trapped in the processing system. Moreover, the initial emotions, perceptions, and physical feelings existing at the time of the trauma may also be trapped, and can be triggered by events in the present. The result can be a range of psychological problems, including anxiety and depression, difficulties relating to others, phobias, panic attacks, and more. Dr. Shapiro includes what she calls "small t" traumas, which are events that leave us with the inability to reprocess negative beliefs about ourselves. These include being teased in school, ridiculed by a parent, or getting lost as a child in a public place.

During EMDR therapy, a client works with a specially trained therapist to target the disturbing memories while focusing on an external visual or audio stimulus. Dr. Shapiro suggests that this external stimulus releases memories that have been "trapped" as a result of the trauma. The client is then able to go back and reprocess the information in a more positive, less distressing way.

Initially, the therapist will take a client history to evaluate whether or not EMDR is appropriate. Determining factors include the ability to deal with severe disturbances, the amount of stress in the client's life, and any pre-existing medical conditions, such as heart or eye problems. The therapist is also interested in the client's support network.

Subsequent phases focus on targeting and treating a specific traumatic memory and replacing any negative self-beliefs connected with it, such as "I am worthless," with positive beliefs, such as "I am a great person." To help achieve this, the therapist moves a finger rapidly back and forth in front of the client's face to redirect eye movements that accompany the recalled trauma. Alternatively, the therapist may use moving lights, alternating hand tapping on a surface, or alternating audio tones. This is done until the client no longer identifies with the negative beliefs. Rhythmic patterns may also be employed to release any bodily tension relating to the traumatic memory. Relaxation techniques also are often taught to combat any emotional disturbances that may occur between sessions.

The final phase of treatment re-evaluates the work of previous sessions to determine if progress has been maintained. Once this entire process has been successfully completed, the phases of therapy may be repeated to reprocess other traumatic memories.

After EMDR processing, clients generally report that the emotional distress related to the memory has been eliminated, or greatly decreased, and that they have gained important cognitive insights. Importantly, these emotional and cognitive changes usually result in spontaneous behavioral and personal change, which are further enhanced with standard EMDR procedures. Memories may continue to surface even after the session is completed. Many times the new memories will work themselves out. However, sometimes it is necessary for the new memories to be processed in the next session. (Shapiro, 2002).

APPENDIX E

IN THE BIBLE, THERE ARE MANY TYPES OF DREAMS AND VISIONS

Examples from the chart in "Dreams and Spiritual Growth A Judeo-Christian Way of Dreamwork." (Savary, 1984).

Abraham's dream-vision-Genesis 15:12–21
Jacob's dream-Genesis 28:10–22
Samuel's call-1 Samuel 3:3–14
Eliphaz's dream-Job 4:12–21
Isaiah's call-Isaiah 6:1–13
Ezekiel's call-Ezekiel 1:4–3:3
Ezekiel's vision-Ezekiel 36:1–14
Dreams in the life of Daniel-Daniel 2–4
Shepherd's dream-Luke 2:8–14
Baptism of Jesus-Matthew 3:16–17
Transfiguration-Luke 9:28–36
Paul's conversion-Acts 9:3–9
Paul's night visions-Acts 16:9; 18:9; 23:11; 27:23

Examples from the chart in "Theology of Christian Healing: A Study for Christians in the Healing Professions." (Pierce, 1998).

Dream of Promise-Genesis 15:1
Dream of Warning-Genesis 20:3
Dream of Heaven-Genesis 29:13
Evaluative Dream-Genesis 37:5–8, 9–11, 18–32
Restorative Dream-Genesis 40:9–13
Dreams of Death-Genesis 40:16–19
Dream of Prophecy-Genesis 41:17–32
Waking Dream-Numbers 24:4
Victory Dream-Jude 7:13–14

Dream of Gifts-1 Kings 3:5
Dream of Spiritual Anxiety-Daniel 2:1
Commission Dream-Habakkuk 2:2
Reassurance Dream-Matthew 1:20
Dream of Warning-Matthew 2:12–13, 19–22
Restrictive Dream-Matthew 17:9
Punishment Dream-Luke 1:22
Prayer Dream-Acts 9:10
Comfort Dream-Acts 9:12
Message Dream-Acts 10:3
Infused Knowledge-Acts 11:5
Revelation Dreams or Visions-Revelation 9:17, Isaiah 1:1, Obadiah 1:1, 2 Chronicles 9:29

APPENDIX F

CARE GIVER ROLE OVERLOAD ASSESSMENT

If you notice any of the following warning signs, you may be reaching role overload and should seek assistance. You may be trying to do too much. Ask yourself these questions:

	Yes	No
1. No matter what you do, your care is not enough.		
2. You feel you are the only person in the world enduring this and that you are alone.		
3. You do not have any time or place to be alone for even brief respite.		
4. Family relationships are breaking down because of care giving pressures.		
5. Your care giving duties are interfering with your work and social life (your other roles) to an unacceptable degree.		
6. You realize you are all alone, and doing it all.		
7. You refuse to think of yourself because "that would be selfish."		
8. Your coping methods have become destructive to you: you are overeating/under eating, abusing drugs/alcohol.		
9. There are no more happy times and there is no humor.		
10. Loving and caring have given way to exhaustion and resentment.		
11. You no longer feel good about yourself or take pride in what you are doing.		
12. You feel like a victim.		
13. You dislike the care recipient.		
14. You are constantly angry.		
15. You have anxiety about facing each day and the future.		
16. You feel depressed (sad or blue) which affects your ability to cope.		

17. You have exhaustion making it impossible to complete necessary tasks of the day.	
18. You have sleeplessness caused by constant concern and worry.	
19. You have irritability that triggers negative responses and reactions in others.	
20. You lack concentration, making it difficult to perform usual daily tasks.	

Learn to recognize signs of stress in yourself, and contact your health care professional if you experience these signs on a regular basis.

Reprinted with permission from Michigan State University Nursing department and the University's Family Care team.

BIBLIOGRAPHY

Albert, Susan Witting, Ph.D. Writing from Life: Telling Your Soul's Story. New York:Jeremy P. Tracher/Penguin, 2004.

Johnson, Robert A. *Inner Work: Using Dreams & Active Imagination for Personal Growth.* San Francisco: Harper, 1986.

Johnson, Robert A. *Owning Your Own Shadow: Understanding the Dark Side of the Psyche.* San Francisco: Harper, 1991.

Kelsey, Morton T. *God, Dreams and Revelation: A Christian Interpretation of Dreams.* Revised and Expanded Edition. Minneapolis: Augsburg, 1991.

Koss, M.P. *Hidden rape: Sexual aggression and victimization in the national sample of students in higher education.* In M.A. Pirog-Good & J.E. Stets (Eds.).Violence in dating relationships: Emerging social issues. New York: Praeger, 1988.

May, Herbert G. and Bruce M. Metzger, ed. *The New Oxford Annotated Bible with The Apocrypha* Expanded Study Bible. Revised Standard Version. New York: Oxford University Press, 1973.

Muller, Wayne. *Touching the Divine: Teachings, Meditations, and Contemplations to Awaken Your True Nature.* Boulder: Sounds True, Incorporated, 1994.

Nouwen, Henri, Michael J. Christensen, and Rebecca Laird. *Spiritual Direction: Wisdom for the Long Walk of Faith.* San Francisco: Harper, 2006.

Patterson, Meg. *Hooked? Net: The New Approach to Drug Cure.* London: Faber & Faber. 1986.

Peace, Richard. *Spiritual Autobiography: Discovering and Sharing Your Spiritual Story.* Colorado Springs, Colorado: Navpress, 1998.

Pearce, Iris. Susan Moore, ed. *Theology of Christian Healing: A Study for Christians in the Healing Professions.* Self Published, 1998.

Pearson, Carol S. *The Hero Within: Six Archetypes We Live By.* San Francisco: Harper and Row, 1989.

Phifier, Nan. *Memoirs of the Soul: Writing Your Spiritual Autobiography.* Cincinnati, Ohio: Walking Stick Press, 2002.

Sanford, John A. *Dreams: God's Forgotten Language.* Reprint. San Francisco: Harper, 1989.

Sanford, John A. *The Invisible Partners: How the Male and Female in Each of Us Affects Our Relationships.* New York: Paulist Press, 1980.

Savary, Louis M., et al. *Dreams and Spiritual Growth A Judeo-Christian Way of Dreamwork.* Mahwah, NJ: Paulist Press, 1984.

Shapiro, Francine. *EMDR as an Integrated Psychotherapy Approach: Experts of Diverse Orientations Explore the Paradigm Prism.* Washington, DC: American Psychological Association Books, 2002.

Shapiro, Francine. *Eye Movement Desensitization, and Reprocessing: Basic Principles, Protocols, and Procedures* (2nd ed.). New York: Guilford Press, 2001.

Smith, Mark Eddy. *Tolkien's: Ordinary Virtues.* Dover Grove, Ill: InterVarsity Press, 2002.

The Book of Common Prayer. According to the use of The Episcopal Church. New York: Oxford University Press, 1990.

Wakefield, Dan. *The Story Of Your Life: Writing A Spiritual Autobiography.* Boston: Beacon Press, 1990.

Warshaw, R. *I Never Called It Rape.* New York: Harper Perennial, 1994.

ABOUT THE AUTHOR

Jeanne G. Miller, MSW, LCSW, has been a psychotherapist for over 20 years. She has worked with individuals, families, and groups in a variety of agencies, hospital settings and in private practice. She has provided supervision to other MSW professionals as they were preparing to sit for their licensing exam. She has been a mental health consultant to nursing homes, pain management rehabilitation centers, and adoption agencies. She has been a speaker at workshops and personal retreat weekends. In her church ministry, she serves as a prayer warrior in the Daughter's of The King Order, as a member of the pastoral care assistant team and as a spiritual director. She and her husband, Dolph, live in Tyler, Texas on a small lake enjoying the beauty of nature. Her hobbies are hiking and photography. Jeanne and Dolph share three children.

Jeanne Miller is available for speaking engagements. Contact her by postal mail at P.O. Box 6907, Tyler, Texas 75711–6907.

Tate Publishing & *Enterprises*

Tate Publishing is committed to excellence in the publishing industry. Our staff of highly trained professionals, including editors, graphic designers, and marketing personnel, work together to produce the very finest books available. The company reflects the philosophy established by the founders, based on Psalms 68:11,

"THE LORD GAVE THE WORD AND GREAT WAS THE COMPANY OF THOSE WHO PUBLISHED IT."

If you would like further information, please call
1.888.361.9473
or visit our website
www.tatepublishing.com

Tate Publishing & *Enterprises*, LLC
127 E. Trade Center Terrace
Mustang, Oklahoma 73064 USA